Models for Integrated Education

Alternative Programs of Integrated Education in Metropolitan Areas

edited by

Daniel U. Levine
University of Missouri, Kansas City

Charles A. Jones Publishing Company
Worthington, Ohio

Contemporary Education Issues
National Society for the Study of Education

Farewell to Schools??? Daniel U. Levine and
Robert J. Havighurst, Editors

Models for Integrated Education, Daniel U.
Levine, Editor

Accountability in Education, Leon M. Lessinger
and Ralph W. Tyler, Editors

Pygmalion Reconsidered, Janet D. Elashoff and
Richard E. Snow

Reactions to Silberman's CRISIS IN THE CLASSROOM,
A. Harry Passow, Editor

This book was prepared in cooperation with the Center for the Study
of Metropolitan Problems in Education and the Experienced Teacher
Fellowship Program of the University of Missouri-Kansas City.

78-407-42

1 2 3 4 5 6 7 8 9 10 / 76 75 74 73 72

Library of Congress Catalog Card Number: 70-184312
International Standard Book Number: 0-8396-0016-X

Printed in the United States of America

Series Foreword

Models for Integrated Education is one of a group of five pub-
lications which constitute the first of a series published under the
auspices of the National Society for the Study of Education. Other
titles are:

> *Farewell to Schools???* edited by Daniel U. Levine and
> Robert J. Havighurst
>
> *Accountability in Education* edited by Leon M. Lessinger
> and Ralph W. Tyler
>
> *Pygmalion Reconsidered* by Janet D. Elashoff and Richard E.
> Snow
>
> *Reactions to Silberman's CRISIS IN THE CLASSROOM* edited
> by A. Harry Passow

For more than seventy years the National Society has published
a distinguished series of Yearbooks. Under an expanded publication program, beginning with the items referred to above, the
Society plans to provide additional services to its members and to
the profession generally. The plan is to publish each year a series
of volumes in paperback form dealing with current issues of concern to educators. The volumes will undertake to present not only
systematic analyses of the issues in question but also varying view-
points with regard to them. In this manner the National Society
expects regularly to supplement its program of Yearbook publication with timely material relating to crucial issues in education.

In this volume Professor Levine has included several original
accounts of various working approaches to integrated education in
metropolitan areas across the country; the descriptions are especially timely.

The National Society for the Study of Education wishes to ac-
knowledge its appreciation to all who have had a part in the preparation of this book.

Kenneth J. Rehage
for the Committee on the Expanded Publication
Program of the National Society for the Study of
Education

Contributors

John Bristol, assistant superintendent in charge of curriculum and instruction, Niles (Illinois) Township Community High School

Edgar G. Epps, Marshall Field Professor of Urban Education, University of Chicago

Denver C. Fox, principal, San Diego City and County School Camps

Herman R. Goldberg, staff member, U. S. Office of Education

Betty Hall, doctoral candidate in counseling, School of Education, University of Missouri at Kansas City

Raymond S. Iman, coordinator of Urban Funded Programs, Rochester Public Schools

Leonard S. Kidd, principal, Fremont and Washington Elementary Schools, San Diego

Robert R. Lentz, educational programs coordinator, OUTWARD BOUND, Inc.

Daniel U. Levine, teaching staff, University of Missouri at Kansas City, currently Fulbright professor, Athens, Greece

Gordon Marker, director, research and consulting firm, Cambridge, Massachusetts

Lloyd J. Mendelson, director, Project Wingspread, Chicago Public Schools

Robert Peebles, Dr. Peebles is the director, Education Collaborative for Greater Boston, lecturer on problems in urban education, Harvard University

Erwin W. Pollack, director, Ray Learning Center, Supplementary Drop-Out Prevention Program, Ethical Humanist Society of Chicago

Albert Stembridge, director, Project APEX, Los Angeles

Meyer Weinberg, editor, *Integrated Education* journal

Preface

Models for Integrated Education was being prepared while the nation waited for the U.S. Supreme Court to determine how much initiative school boards must take in desegregating public schools. On April 20, 1971, the Court ruled that school officials in southern and border states would have to take affirmative remedial measures, including the transporation of students, to "eliminate from the public schools all vestiges of state-imposed segregation," even though laws originally establishing segregation had long since been rescinded.

The Court did not provide much definite guidance concerning the elimination or reduction of segregated schools originating in segregated housing patterns, particularly in metropolitan areas of the north where black students tend to be concentrated in central city schools and white students are concentrated in predominantly white suburbs. Even if subsequent Court decisions require that big city school districts take affirmative action to reduce segregation within their own boundaries, the possibility that the courts will require desegregation across district boundaries within the foreseeable future seems quite remote. Given the segregated housing patterns in most metropolitan areas, it is obvious that many white and black children will continue to be denied integrated educational experiences unless voluntary efforts are made to bring young people of different backgrounds together in the schools.

Fortunately, there is much that can be done to give students of different racial, social, and ethnic backgrounds meaningful opportunities to share educational experiences even when residential segregation by race and social class makes it difficult to attend traditional neighborhood schools together. President Richard M. Nixon called attention to such possibilities in a major policy statement on education (March 24, 1970) in which he said:

. . . Rather than attempting dislocation of whole schools, a portion of a child's educational activities may be shared with children from other schools. Some of this education is in a "home-base" school, but some outside of it. This "outside learning" is in settings that are defined neither as black nor white, and sometimes in settings that are not even traditional school buildings. It may range all the way from intensive work in reading to training in technical skills, and to joint efforts such as drama and athletics.

On May 21, 1970 the president wrote a letter to Congress in support of his request for approval of the Emergency School Assistance Act, reaffirming his earlier statement on the importance of overcoming interracial and intercultural isolation:

It is in the national interest that where such isolation exists, even though it is not of a kind that violates the law, we should do our best to assist local school districts attempting to overcome its effects . . .

This Act deals specifically with problems which arise from racial separation, whether deliberate or not, and whether past or present. It is clear that racial isolation ordinarily has an adverse effect on education. Conversely, we also know that desegregation is vital to quality education— not only from the standpoint of raising the achievement levels of the disadvantaged, but also from the standpoint of helping all children achieve the broad-based human understanding that increasingly is essential in today's world. . .

Few issues facing us as a nation are of such transcendent importance; important because of the vital role that our public schools play in the nation's life and in its future; because the welfare of our children is at stake; because our national conscience is at stake, and because it presents us a test of our capacity to live together in one nation, in brotherhood and understanding.

The president's comments were encouraging to educators and others who had been pointing out for years that integrated education may be a precondition for national survival. It is true that parts of the message provided some reinforcement for the myths propagated by those white and black separatists who see integrated education either as "burdening" white children or "patronizing" black children. Elsewhere, however, the president's emphasis was on the "transcendent importance" of integrated education for the nation as a whole.

Several bills have been introduced in Congress for the purpose of providing financial assistance to reduce segregation in the schools. For example, H.R. 19446, passed by the House of Representatives during the waning hours of the 1970 session, would have made one and one-half billion dollars available in fiscal 1971 and 1972 "to encourage the voluntary elimination, reduction, or prevention of racial isolation in elementary and secondary schools with substantial proportions of minority group students." Senate bill 1557, approved by the Senate on April 26, 1971 following one of the most dramatic debates in that chamber's history, authorized an appropriation of a similar amount to be spent by June 30, 1973 on efforts to reduce the isolation of minority students in the schools.

If Congress does made substantial amounts of money available for school desegregation, what exactly can school districts do to initiate "innovative interracial educational projects" (H.R. 19446) and establish "quality integrated schools" (S. 1557)? Most educators have had little experience with such projects. The basic purpose of this book is to provide illustrations of feasible alternatives for pluralistic schooling which might be adopted by local school districts.

The programs described are not the only exciting and innovative programs now being conducted which combine academic, intercultural, and other educational goals. Nor are they necessarily the best, though they certainly are among the best. All of them are innovative and exemplary in the sense that they successfully strive to attain one or more additional fundamental educational goals such as improvement in academic instruction, familiarization with the affairs of a metropolitan area, and enhancement of identity through experiences that challenge young people to set high standards of accomplishment for themselves. Each illustrates a type of pluralistic (or potentially pluralistic) educational setting that should be eminently eligible for federal funding.

To highlight some of the lessons we believe can be learned from this book and to avoid possible misunderstandings, a few additional comments are made here concerning features common to many of the programs described.

1) If interracial education is valuable not only for minority students but for all students and for the nation as a whole, then it follows that efforts should be made to design programs which do not place a special burden on any particular group of students. Inasmuch as some observers believe that programs which bus inner city black students to predominantly white schools in middle-class neighborhoods do constitute such a burden, account should be taken of this perception whenever possible. Such busing may be justified by the need to reduce concentrations of low-income children in inner city schools, but at the very least, school districts which sponsor one-way busing simultaneously should institute other types of programs which bring students of different backgrounds together in central

locations. The latter types of programs also yield substantial additional benefits such as improvement in instruction through educational technology.

2) None of the programs described in this book allows students to be brought together within a school only to be kept consistently separated by tracking, homogenous grouping, or other policies which result in segregation within classrooms. While there legitimately may be occasions when students of one race may work together on an assignment of special interest, "caucus" together, or otherwise temporarily constitute a uniracial group, in general it mocks the purposes of interracial education to desegregate a school but not integrate its classrooms.

3) There is an urgent need for continuous monitoring and evaluation. Since special problems are likely to be encountered in educational programs which are innovative and controversial, formative as well as summative evaluation components should be provided. If difficulties are identified as soon as they appear there is a better chance that they can be eliminated. Many examples of useful evaluation approaches are given in the various chapters.

4) Programs of the type illustrated should not be viewed as full or adequate answers to the problems of racial isolation in our schools or society. On the one hand, it is true that they represent substantial advances over most existing school programs in facilitating inter-group contact, in using community resources for learning, in instituting more flexible scheduling and organization in the schools, in providing copportunities for outdoor education and character-building. On the other hand, it is also true that in many cases they bring students together only for a relatively short ime and do not provide sequential opportunities for interracial experience throughout childhood and adolescence. Such programs represent more a foundation upon which to build than a pinnacle on which to rest. It would be tragic if educators and concerned laymen were to neglect the dangers forcefully expressed by Senator Abraham Ribicoff of Connecticut in Senate debate on the emergency school-aid bills, as well as on his own bill requiring affirmative action for metropolitan desegregation:

No one can argue that our school systems throughout the country do not need the $1,500,000,000 authorized by this legislation. In city after city we see the specter of schools and school districts going bankrupt financially as well as educationally . . .

But, unfortunately, I think the integration promised by this bill will prove a will-o'-the-wisp. Concerned citizens across the country, white and black, will look to this bill as a national attack on racial isolation—and they will be quickly and sharply disappointed. The integration in this bill is only a charade. It is simply more of the same as far as the basic problem is concerned. . . .this bill does nothing to attack the problem of segregation where it is most virulent—in the relationship between the suburbs and central cities across our country.

Our cities are increasingly populated by minority groups and our suburbs take on the character of an encircling white noose. Our schools, drawing pupils as a consequence of geography, follow suit.

We used to think that segregation in America was a problem of one region, the South. . .We thought the problem was confined primarily to our schools but now we know the cancer goes to the heart of our society.

We only delude ourselves and imperil our future by thinking that the suburbs will be able to insulate themselves from the decay and suffering of the central cities. We will all soon be infected and overcome by the disease unless we take steps to eradicate it.

It is possible that programs of the kind described in the following pages will draw the attention of some away from the long-range problems posed by segregation in the metropolitan area. If Senator Ribicoff's worst fears are not to be realized, it is vitally important that pluralistic school programs be seen as but one step toward the ultimate goal of reversing metropolitan patterns which generate hatreds by isolating racial and social groups from another and obscuring their common interest in achieving the ideal of unity amidst diversity.

Daniel U. Levine

Contents

Chapter

I. Introduction: Race and Educational Opportunity, *Meyer Weinberg* 1

II. Project *Unique* and Efforts to Eliminate Racial Imbalance in Rochester, New York, *Herman R. Goldberg and Raymond S. Iman* 7

Inner City-Outer City and Other Programs Within the District, 8
Open Enrollment and Magnet School Programs, 8; Triad Zoning Plan, 10
Urban-Suburban Transfer Plan, 12
Suburban Participation in Irondequoit, 12; History and Expansion, 14; Evaluation, 17
Project Unique: The World of Inquiry School, 18
World of Inquiry School, 19
Summary, 23

III. Project *Apex*: Magnet Schools for Enrichment and Exchange in Los Angeles, *Albert W. Stembridge* 24

Objectives of the Project, 25
Components of the Project, 25
University Involvement, 25; Community Involvement, 27; Guidance and Counseling Component, 27; Voluntary Student Exchange Component, 28
Evaluation of the Program, 28
Summary and Conclusion, 30

IV. Chicago's School Without Walls: The Chicago Public High School for Metropolitan Studies, *Edgar G. Epps* 32

Instructional Program, 33
Implementation, 35
Facilities, 35;
Informality, 37; Student Selection, 37; Teacher Selection, 38
Plans for Evaluation, 39
Summary, 41

V. Intergroup Relationships in a School Camp Environment, *Denver C. Fox*   43

    The Outdoor Education Program, 43
    The Camping Program, 44
    Intergroup Relationships in the Camp Program, 45
    A Look Ahead, 47

VI. A Learning Center in an Integrated Elementary School, *Erwin Pollack*   49

    Background of the Project, 49
    How the Learning Center Operates, 51
    Special Projects and Events, 54
    Help for Individual Pupils, 55
    Conclusion, 56

VII. Urban-Suburban Collaboration: The EdCo Experience, *Robert W. Peebles and Gordon A. Marker*   58

    What Is EdCo? 59
    The EdCo Model, 59
    Teacher Services, 60
    Student Services, 62
    Special Services, 63
    Summary, 64

VIII. A Summer School for Understanding Metropolitan Living, *Daniel U. Levine and Betty Hall*   66

    The Goals of the Program, 67
    Evaluation of the UML, 70
       Student Reactions, 70; Parent Reactions, 71; Teacher Reactions, 72; Interracial Relationships in UML, 73
    Comments and Recommendations, 74

IX. Outward Bound—Education Through Experience, *Robert R. Lentz*   77

    The Program, 78
    The Make-up of the Group—Some Apparent Lessons, 82
    Programs Run in Affiliation with Outward Bound—Some Examples, 84
       East High School, Denver, Colorado, 84; Trenton High School, Action Bound Program, 86
    Conclusion, 88

X. Individualization and Non-Grading in an Integrated Elementary School, *Leonard S. Kidd*   89

    Model School Program, 90
    Summer Workshop Program, 91
    Individualized Learning, 93
    Learning Resource Center, 94
    Program Evaluation, 96

XI. Project Wingspread: The Chicago Area City-Suburban Exchange Program,
Lloyd J. Mendelson and John Bristol   98

    Growth of Project Wingspread, 1968-1970, 99
    Programs, 99
        Direct School Exchange Pairings, 99; The Magnet or Central Site, 99; Once-a-Week Interest Groups, 100
    Staffing and Implementation, 100
    Curriculum and Instruction, 101
    Wingspread: A Suburban View, 103
    Problems, 104
        Apprehensive City and Suburban Parents, 104; Tensions and Hostilities Resulting from Racial Isolation and Stereotypes, 105; Differences in Teaching Approaches and Attitudes Toward Learning Among Teamed Teachers, 105
    Evaluation, 105
    Additional Impact and Implications, 107

XII. From Model to Practice: Guidelines for the Effective Implementation of Interracial Programs,
Daniel U. Levine   109

I

Introduction:
Race and
Educational
Opportunity

Meyer Weinberg

Race has been part of the curriculum ever since we have had
public schools. Before the Civil War American schools accepted
and perpetuated racist values. Textbooks treated blacks and other
minorities as undesirables. Blacks were often excluded from public
schools—North and South—and, when admitted, frequently forced
to sit in a separate part of the classroom.

After the destruction of slavery, exclusion and/or denigration of
minority values continued. Except for a moment of enlightenment
during Reconstruction, the years 1870-1920 were a low point in the
history of American race relations.

During the past half-century, interracial attendance has become
a reality in many schools. Today, one-seventh of all children attend
an interracial or interethnic public school. Yet the heritage of the
past still weighs heavily upon the American classroom. Practices
originally created to serve racist purposes linger on as thoughtless
monuments to the past. Textbooks remain largely untouched by
newer currents of thought. The curriculum is still inadequately re-
sponsive to recent research, especially in the social sciences. But the
greatest impediment to essential change is the ethnic isolation that
still characterizes the American classroom.

Over the past fifty years, interracial education has taken several
forms. The human relations approach evolved during the 1920's

and held the field, so to speak, for a generation. The method essentially was based on the concept of tolerance. It was a defensive teaching strategy, aimed principally at counter-balancing an overbearing majority sentiment which rejected equally differences of color, language, and national custom. Much attention was paid to explaining cultural peculiarities.

Interpersonal conflict was seen as a clash of single individuals. Prejudice was regarded as a failing of individuals who lacked an ability to see others as individuals. It was hoped that this lack could be remedied by the acquisition of information about the minority person. The minority person, in turn, was regarded as a passive object, too weak to prevail against the majority; thus, the human relations approach was inevitably moralistic in its appeal.

A second approach may be called interracial. This method frankly acknowledged the fact of anti-Negro prejudice and distinguished it from the area of simple culture conflict. The unique role of the Negro in American life was seen as a central distinguishing characteristic of American society. Concern with individual prejudice extended now to exploration of discrimination. Disability and deprivation were found to be aspects of group existence in America. Negroes were seen as a sub-culture with its own distinctive development. Great efforts were expended on discovering the manifold forms of group discrimination against Negroes and Indians especially. Discrimination against Negroes was found to be far more resistant than that based on religion, language, or national origin.

In the classroom, spreading celebration of events such as Negro History Week illustrated the fact of separate existence. It also signalled an affirmation of Negro accomplishment and initiative. To be sure, it was in the segregated black classroom that the celebration was most likely to adopt such a tone. Only in occasional large urban schools, integrated in some sense, were similar events celebrated.

The interracial approach was more realistic than the human relations approach, though it was also defensive in orientation. Children were taught the disability of color in American life. But they failed to learn to conceive of a world without this disability. So far-fetched did such a world seem that the possibility was not discussed.

Today, a third approach—the human rights approach—is in the making. This method presents group differences affirmatively, and its ideology is an unshrinking proclamation of universal equality. Essentially, it is a belief that members of ethnic groups have the absolute right to define their own ethnic status: They will be what they decide. It is neither separatism nor desegregation but pluralism with equality. The goal is not to be like or with others on principle.

Assimilation is rejected because it assumes lack of worth on the part of the minority. Increasingly, however, the group is viewed in terms of its dignity. (*Dignus* is Latin for "worth.") Integration as such is rejected as too prescriptive for everyone; instead it becomes one other option that some minority people can select—if they wish. In fact, of course, the option to integrate has almost always remained a white prerogative. Pluralism without equality, as Kenneth B. Clark has noted, is hardly more than a caste system, where each sub-culture has the right to exist so long as it keeps its "place."

The new movement for human rights thus strains at the seams of the traditional racial order. Even national boundaries are overtaken. If the object now is to win those rights that are common to all mankind, then a world-wide bond comes to bind all men together. The movement for human rights is therefore internationalist as well; consequently, one hears of a Third World—a combination of people in the former European colonies along with black Americans, Mexican-Americans, Indian-Americans, and Asian-Americans.

None of the approaches discussed above is unconnected with the others. One may stress cultural distinctiveness in any of them. It will, however, take much hard thought by school people to formulate an effective response to the challenge of human rights. Some may be put off by the very newness of the subject. Alas! We cannot wait until this subject "settles down." It is up to us to create the instructional strategies and materials. This is the purpose of the present book.

What may we expect from heightened attention to racial and ethnic matters in the classroom? What are the educative consequences of interracial experiences? A good deal of research has gone on already and the findings are very encouraging. Following are a series of generalizations made on the basis of a large number of studies of desegregation experiences.

1) Academic achievement rises as the minority child learns more while the advantaged majority child continues to learn at his accustomed rate. The achievement gap thus narrows. This finding is, for all practical purposes, established in relation to black children. It is less firm with regard to Indian-Americans and Mexican-American children.

2) Negro aspirations, already high, are positively affected; self-esteem rises; and self-acceptance as a Negro grows. With some exceptions, this is firmly established for Negro children; indicated for Mexican-American children; and true in an indeterminate degree for Indian-American children.

3) Toleration, respect, and occasional friendships are the chief characteristics of student and teacher relations in the desegre-

gated school. Little informal socializing occurs outside school. Exceptions are numerous with physical violence playing a fluctuating role. When a school is not stably desegregated but is in the process of transition from all-majority to all-minority, instability is often associated with violence.

4) While culturally different from the Negro-Americans, the Indian-Americans and Mexican-Americans do not seem to respond to desegregation in any culturally unique ways.

5) The Coleman Report and the U.S. Commission on Civil Rights Study of Racial Isolation lend support to the learning and attitudinal effects of desegregation.

6) The effects of desegregation on black Americans are evident; the support the Negro community lends to desegregation is widespread. The movement toward black nationalism has thus far, at least, not produced mass disillusionment with the value of desegregation. The only mass movement among blacks in the United States today is taking place in numerous southern towns and cities on behalf of an equitable form of desegregation, not separatism.

7) Virtually none of the negative predictions by anti-desegregationists finds support in studies of actual desegregation. The rejected predictions concern lower achievement, aggravated self-concepts of Negro children, and growing disorder in desegregated schools, stable or transitional.

Several, at least, of the foregoing findings deserve to be examined in more detail. One issue, much discussed, involves the relative role of race and social class. The Coleman Report stressed the importance of class, the Racial Isolation Study also stressed the importance of race. Social scientists have been reluctant to grant an autonomous importance to race. This seems ill-advised. Americans have traditionally been separated by race with momentous psychological consequences for both segregator and segregated. It would be extraordinary if these consequences stopped at the school door. Undoubtedly, however, social class is a more fundamental factor, crossing, as it does, all racial lines. Perhaps the safest way to summarize the point is to say that separating race from class is as difficult as separating the red from the white in pink. If black children suffer deprivation in their school, it is probable that this results from a combination of race and class. Desegregation across both racial and social class lines would seem to promise the most benefits.

An integrated school is one in which equal opportunity is realized in fact through deliberate cooperation and without regard to artificial barriers confronting the child. The key word is *realized*. An integrated school is not one in which equality is preached while inequality is practiced. Nor is it a school in which education is equally poor for everyone. Integration requires an instructional strategy that deals with the educational needs of individual children. And it calls for a genuine commitment to academic achievement. Without either feature, the school may be a desegregated failure. (Note, however, that no integration is possible in the absence of desegregation.)

Much is heard nowadays about raising the self-concept of black children. Implied are contentions that 1) their self-concept is poor and 2) self-concept and oppression are inversely related. Both these contentions frequently prove incorrect.

If high Negro self-concept and aspiration are only recent discoveries of social scientists, it is not because they only recently arose. Cox points out: "Even as far back as the days of slavery Negro aspiration was everywhere evident. We could not conceive of any institution of hope, such as the Negro spirituals, developing among the lower castes of India. . . ."(1) Bond explained sardonically years ago: "For it is self-respect that gives to the American Negro that inner security in the face of real or fancied injuries which was accorded him as a member of a group definitely in its place."(2) A contemporary researcher, Coopersmith, accounts for the coexistence of oppression and high self-esteem: " . . . It is not discrimination *per se* but the person's acceptance of his oppressor's judgment and standards, and rejection of his own standards that is likely to produce self-devaluation."(3)

Guggenheim studied self-esteem among children in Harlem. He reported that low self-esteem appeared not to be a problem. Then he proceeded to an important practical application of his findings: "The results of this study certainly raise a question concerning the validity of pre-kindergarten and elementary school programs for disadvantaged Negro children that have as a primary goal the raising of self esteem. . . Strong evidence from this and other studies . . . indicate(s) . . . that many disadvantaged Negro children's school problems center around low achievement and not low self-esteem."(4)

Coopersmith takes a step beyond: "It may be that pride evocation is a rapid procedure for gaining esteem, and if so, may well serve as a first step in programs to increase initiative and motivation. However, unless esteem is subsequently related to skills, performance, etc., the motivation aroused may be socially unproductive."(5)

Some time ago, Erikson explored this question with great wisdom. Two aspects of the general subject of identity are of interest here: a) its substantive content and b) its social-psychological dimensions. Both are illustrated by the following statements by Erikson: "In this, children cannot be fooled by empty praise and condescending encouragement. They may have to accept artificial bolstering of their self-esteem in lieu of something better, but what I call their accruing ego identity gains real strength only from wholehearted and consistent recognition of real accomplishment, that is, achievement that has meaning in their culture."(6)

And further: "Identity formation goes beyond the process of identifying oneself with ideal others in a one-way fashion; it is a process based on a heightened cognitive and emotional capacity to let oneself be identified by concrete persons as a circumscribed individual in relation to a predictable universe which transcends the family."(7)

To what extent does Erikson illuminate contemporary efforts to raise black self-esteem through Negro history and black culture? Where these efforts are substitutes for genuine achievement in basic cognitive areas, they seem actuated largely by condescension. Through much of the more recent literature on self-esteem appears the emphasis upon the cognitive dimension. Without such a consideration, we are left with hardly more than esteem-uplift. (One of the undoubted advantages of such programs is their low cost—in money, if not in human promise.)

School integration has travelled a familiar road from heated partisan issue to accepted public policy. Educators are now asked to take another great step forward by translating high principle into everyday educational practice. The contents of this volume are designed to suggest desirable directions although they are by no means exhaustive. The authors of individual chapters are to be congratulated for their ingenuity and courage. Thoreau once said that he could hardly wait to finish reading a good book because he wanted so to get up and put it into practice. This is that kind of book.

Notes

(1) Oliver C. Cox, *Caste, Class and Race: A Study in Social Dynamics* (New York: *Monthly Review Press,* 1959, orig. 1948).
(2) Horace Mann Bond, "Self-Respect as a Factor in Racial Advancement," *Annals* 140 (1928):23.
(3) Stanley Coopersmith, *Psychological Deprivation and the Development of Self-Esteem: Comments and Recommendations* (Bethesda, Md.: National Institute of Child Health and Human Development, 1968), p. 9.
(4) Fred Guggenheim, "Self-Esteem and Achievement Expectations for White and Negro Children," *Journal of Projective Techniques and Personality Assessment* 33 (1969):70.
(5) Coopersmith, *op. cit.,* p. 15.
(6) Erik H. Erikson, "A Memorandum of Identity and Negro Youth," *Journal of Social Issues* 20 (1964):32.
(7) *Ibid.,* p. 33.

II

Project *Unique* and Efforts to Eliminate Racial Imbalance in Rochester, New York

Herman R. Goldberg
and Raymond S. Iman

In the early 1960's, a detailed study of the Rochester, New York, City School District revealed there was no significant difference between inner city black and outer city white schools if the comparison were limited to class size, quality of teachers, inservice education, condition of school building, number and location of transportable classrooms, supplies and special services, and teacher attendance. Pupil achievement and attendance, however, were in some instances, measurably lower in inner city schools. A critical examination of school policies and administrative decision in Rochester clearly revealed that neither contributed to racial imbalance in the schools. Existing housing patterns, lack of alternative public policy on housing, and adherence to the neighborhood school concept were the factors which determined the racial composition of a school's student body.

Berefit of political power, inner city residents in Rochester and most other metropolitan centers were ill-equipped to force the power structure to alter either the housing arrangements or the racial composition of ghetto schools. They resorted to the same vehicle used in the south, the courts. In May of 1962, a civil action suit was filed against the Rochester Board of Education in the Western District of the U. S. District Court. With the support of

7

court decisions from other sections of the United States, the citizens demanded alterations in the traditional residence requirements that prevented children from attending schools outside their neighborhood.

Many plans were being considered in Rochester in 1964 when a massive civil disturbance erupted. Although the widespread destruction had a positive catalytic effect on the implementation of some of the proposals, it is pertinent to note that interest in the problem of racial imbalance antedated by at least a year the destructive street disturbances which occurred during the summer of 1964. A modest but important step forward was taken during the summer of 1963 when four high schools were designated as summer school centers. All residential requirements were eliminated and pupils were permitted to select any center. Course offerings were based on student requests and teacher assignments were made without regard to the teacher's location during the school year.

Rochester's efforts to eliminate racial imbalance received strong support in September of 1963 when Dr. James E. Allen Jr., at that time New York State Commissioner of Education, requested all school districts to submit: 1) a statement on racial imbalance (i.e., all schools with a student body that was more than 50% non-white); 2) a statement of board policy on imbalance; 3) a report of progress toward eliminating it; 4) a plan for further action that would include cost and time estimates.

The Rochester City School District's response to demands for desegregation from both the state and the community were intensive as well as extensive. Programs were designed and implemented in three major areas: (1) plans which involved inner city and outer city schools within the Rochester School District; (2) development of an urban-suburban transfer program; and (3) creation of Project UNIQUE (United Now for Integrated Quality Urban-Suburban Education).

Inner City-Outer City and Other Programs Within the District

Open Enrollment and Magnet School Programs

The Rochester Board of Education passed a resolution on November 21, 1963, directing the City School District's administrative staff to initiate plans to implement an "Open Enrollment Plan." Six schools which had the highest percentage of racial imbalance (eighty to ninety percent non-white) were designated as sending schools. Eighteen schools with a non-white enrollment which was lower than the city-wide average were identified as receiving schools.

On December 2, 1963, less than a month after the directive from the Board, parents of every pupil in the sending schools received a letter asking if they were interested in having their child transferred to one of the receiving schools. The response was overwhelming: 1,500 acceptances were received by the Central Office. It became immediately apparent that there was not enough room for all who wanted to participate. To avoid the problems involved in a mid-year shift of pupil population, all of the 1,500 transfer applicants were carefully screened. A detailed "inventory" was made of eighteen outer city elementary schools and places were found for 513 applicants. Attrition proved to be exceedingly modest and 495 completed the school year in their new school and 480 pupils returned to their newly assigned school the next fall.

The open enrollment program, however, involved only about 1% of the total school population. As a pioneering effort in the reversal of traditional pupil enrollment patterns, it was of historic importance, but it did not involve enough numbers of children. The numerical limit of open enrollment was dictated by the availability of space in outer city schools. In an attempt to circumvent this barrier, the superintendent announced a new policy.

Two of the relatively new elementary schools in the inner city were classified as "open" schools, and parents from the outer city were asked to transfer their children and thus convert the open enrollment plan to a two-way street. This innovative program could not be sold by pamphlets and pleas alone; it had to be sold either on a one-to-one basis or through personal discussions with small groups. Central office personnel, led by the superintendent and equipped with a slide presentation, embarked on the tedious and time-consuming task of selling the community. Evening meetings and coffee hours were held in the homes of interested groups of parents. A nucleus of support gradually was created and some parents agreed to permit their children to participate. The numbers slowly increased, and by September 1967, 140 children from 30 predominantly white schools were attending Clara Barton School No. 2—a "magnet" inner city school. Included in this group were the children of important community leaders and professionals. Enrichment programs were added in 1968. Special instruction in mathematics and science, remedial reading, French, a Far Eastern Studies program, and Project Beacon (a black studies ego development program) were among the major additions.

In response to the criticism by Negro parents that school administrators were unduly attentive to the needs and wishes of the participating whites, a racially integrated parents' group was created. Among the major achievements of this new association of parents was the addition of a hot lunch program for the school. An important by-product of the group was the creation of the Committee for Expanded School Integration, which urged whites and blacks to increase their participation in the two-way voluntary transfer plan. This dual approach constituted a partial response to those who insisted that "the blacks are doing all the moving."

Clara Barton School No. 2 now has 240 white children and a waiting list of 170. The teachers enjoy the new "mix," and it is reflected in their enthusiasm, *esprit de corps,* and performance. Those who predicted a decline in pupil achievement because of the new racial composition were refuted by the evaluation conclusions:

1) White children who voluntarily transferred into an inner city school and those who remained in their neighborhood schools achieved at the same level during the year.
2) Negro pupils achieved better when in integrated classes in the same inner city school than when in classes almost completely Negro in enrollment.
3) Negro pupils achieved better when in larger classes that were integrated than when in smaller classes almost completely Negro in enrollment.

Open enrollment has made impressive gains since its introduction in 1963-64 when 495 participated in the program. During the 1970-71 school year 1,020 were involved in elementary open enrollment (inner city to outer); 320 pupils participated in secondary school open enrollment; 185 white pupils from the outer city attended an inner city school. Every school in the city now has some Negro children in attendance.

There is more to integrating schools than moving children. Teachers in receiving schools must be prepared for some of the adjustments that are necessary if the program is to expand successfully. Some teachers developed the unfortunate habit of referring to "our children" and "their children." This distasteful distinction has now disappeared.

Bus routes and schedules are revised as needed to improve service. A special inservice program was developed for bus matrons to improve their rapport with children. New insights and improved handling of pupil incidents were noted following the training sessions.

Triad Zoning Plan

Another approach to the problem of racial imbalance is the Voluntary Extended Home Zone, or Triad Plan. Three contiguous neighborhood schools were grouped together to make one attendance zone instead of three. Children from this enlarged zone could apply to go to any one of the three schools. However, children who live in the home school zone were not displaced. One hundred fiftynine children received access to a different school through this plan. An important feature of the program is that the Triad Plan helps to preserve the basic values of the traditional neighborhood school policy and at the same time meets the objection that the neighborhood policy, rigidly adhered to, supports and preserves racial segregation. Under this plan the neighborhood is enlarged rather than destroyed and children may transfer to one of the other schools in the zone, which is still within walking distance of their homes.

The results have been encouraging. An important part of the educational process of convincing parents occurred in familytype seminars where parents and children together discussed the idea, and ideally were exposed to the broader social issues involved. Such concomitant learnings are central to the success of the program.

At the time of the adoption of the Triad Plan only the most prophetic observers realized that it would constitute an important interim step for the December 1969 report on "Grade Reorganization and Desegregation of the Rochester Public Schools." The addition of one school to each of two of the three original Triad zones made the groupings proposed in the reorganization plan racially balanced. Thus the planning effort exerted on behalf of Triad proved to be an extremely valuable intermediate step when the school district formulated a plan for complete desegregation.

The need for additional facilities enabled the school district to move in another direction in the attack on racial imbalance. Frederick Douglass Junior High School, a new school on the outer rim of the city, was completed and ready for occupancy in September 1968. In the absence of established feeder patterns, it was possible to create a student body that was racially balanced at the outset. Despite strong objections from parents whose children were not included in the new feeder pattern, the initial plan survived with only minor modifications. If housing patterns remain relatively stable, this junior high school will remain racially balanced. Scheduled construction of new junior high schools in other sections of Rochester will enable the school district to maintain racial balance because the burdens of precedent are either non-existent or much less venerable.

In addition to these programs which provide access to other schools, services to inner city schools have increased sharply. Some of the best teaching is being conducted in disadvantaged neighborhoods. More teachers have asked to be transferred into these schools than out of them. Sizable pre-school programs, development of vocational and occupational opportunities, and stepped-up compensatory programs also were made available at the same time Open Enrollment and the Triad Plan were started.

Urban-Suburban Transfer Plan

The racial statistics for schools in the United States and for those in Monroe County, N. Y. (Rochester and its suburbs) are depressingly similar. Almost 80 percent of the white students in the United States attend schools that are more than 91 percent white and more than 54 percent of all Negro students attend schools that are more than 90 percent black.

In Monroe County, more than 95 percent of the whites attend schools that have a Negro enrollment of less than 5 percent and 54 percent of the Negroes are enrolled in schools where more than 70 percent of the pupils are black. This relatively high degree of racial imbalance is difficult to defend when one examines the population density of the county. No suburb is more than 15 miles from the center of Rochester; this proximity sharply reduces the logistical problems that are frequently associated with urban-suburban transfer programs.

There is little evidence to support the conclusion that racial attitudes in Monroe County are basically different from those found in many other metropolitan areas. Despite the presence of small, isolated, albeit growing pockets of socially conscious citizens, the prevailing point of view among many residents continues to present a formidable obstacle to the achievement of meaningful action in altering racial imbalance in Rochester's schools.

Suburban Participation in Irondequoit

The Urban-Suburban Transfer program is not a statistical exercise in which children become numbers and groups become totals. Our hope is to alter the present trend toward racial polarization by reducing racial imbalance in both urban and suburban schools. White racism is a strong barrier to this goal, but there are encouraging signs that this can be overcome. Irondequoit Central School District No. 3, which is located in a Rochester suburb, is an illustration of what can be accomplished by people who are committed to racially balanced schools.

A school in the Rochester area originally was considered racially imbalanced only if its enrollment was more than 50 percent black. Several members of the Board of Education of Irondequoit informally discussed this criterion while in attendance at an educational conference. They concluded that a school that was 99 percent white is just as much a victim of racial imbalance as one that is 99 percent black. The Superintendent of Schools of the City School District was also attending the same conference and a meeting with the full suburban school board was arranged. Preliminary discussions were encouraging and all the participants agreed to meet in Rochester for additional exploratory talks. After careful review of the legal implications, and with the advice and consent of the New York State Education Department and the approval of the Boards of Education in both communities, the pupil transfer was begun in September 1965.

Although the size of the program was modest—only 24 pupils were involved—the breakthrough was crucial. Initial public reaction in Irondequoit was exceedingly antagonistic. The serenity of a suburb had been shattered. Opponents of the program made repeated allusions to the Board's "secrecy." They flatly refused to discuss the merits of the proposal and elected to concentrate their attack on the "method" used.

The first school board election in Irondequoit after the adoption of the plan resulted in the election of three members (of seven on the board) who campaigned on an anti-busing platform. This trend was partially reversed in March 1969 when an aroused segment of the community responded to an attempt by some members of the board to terminate the program. As a result of strong community action and the energetic support of the Irondequoit Teachers Association, the motion to abolish was defeated. A majority of the Board voted to permit the 24 inner city children to continue in the program and later approved a plan to add 25 new pupils in September 1969. School Board elections in June 1969 and in June 1970 resulted in the election of Board members who supported the program. Another extension of the program occurred in September 1970.

The division among residents of the Irondequoit School District provoked considerable acrimonious debate. Voting on school issues increased from 10 percent to about 37 percent of the eligible voters. Supporters of the urban-suburban transfer plan were able to cite Rochester's efforts to achieve racial balance within the City School District. If Rochester had either dragged its feet or concluded that "we can't do it," Irondequoit probably would not have participated in a transfer program. It is completely unrealistic to expect those who are not directly responsible for a program to support it vigorously if the main participants are apathetic.

Proponents of the plan grossly overestimated Irondequoit's concern for racial minorities. In an attempt to increase citizen support for the program in the community, a critical and comprehensive examination of the transfer plan was made by a group of citizens appointed by the board. The conclusions of their report should be required reading for anyone who is considering adoption of a comparable plan. Among the strengths and weaknesses of the transfer plan were: 1) extensive curriculum revision had occurred; 2) opportunities for suburban children to become better acquainted with the several races and cultures of the metropolitan Rochester area had increased; 3) interracial and inter-cultural relations had improved; 4) class size agreements had not been violated; 5) rates of learning in integrated classes had not been affected by the presence of inner city pupils; 6) transfer pupils were performing at least as well as their counterparts in the sending school; 7) bus schedules severely limited participation by city pupils in after school activities; 8) parent involvement had been relatively small; 9) in Irondequoit the strongest support for the program came from teachers and administrators and the parents of children in integrated classrooms, and 10) community sentiment against the program had contributed to the defeat of two out of four budget votes and three of five proposals for land acquisition and building programs.

The committee recommended that a referendum be held to determine whether the transfer program would be continued. It also supported retention of those pupils presently enrolled for at least one more year. Although the committee was created to reduce polarization within the community, the report actually increased division and raised the emotional level of the debate. Members of the Board of Education elected not to implement the recommendation for a referendum, and the election of three pro-transfer board members in June 1969 insured continuation of the exchange program.

This detailed account of the impact of the urban-suburban transfer program in a typical suburban community must not be interpreted as an accurate indication of what necessarily is in the offing for all who attempt to follow a similar plan. Some observers contend that the program would have died if there had been extensive community discussion. Others say there was need for broader involvement on the part of suburban citizens prior to the program's adoption and implementation. The traumatic effect of the transfer plan can be partially explained by the fact that prior to its adoption there were only four blacks in the West Irondequoit school population of 5,800. Acceptance of 24 inner city pupils, even when dispersed among several schools, represented a sharp change from the *status quo*.

History and Expansion

Irondequoit's seminal effort had effects that extended beyond the boundaries of both school districts. Rochester Superintendent of

Schools Herman R. Goldberg met with Dr. William A. Fullagar, who at that time was Dean of the College of Education at the University of Rochester, to discuss ways in which concerned suburbanites could develop an expanded urban-suburban transfer plan. Meetings were arranged with the eighteen suburban superintendents and the city superintendent to discuss all phases of suburban racial isolation and racial imbalance in Rochester. The superintendent made a detailed presentation which included an explanation of Rochester's demography, progress of the Open Enrollment Plan, and a long range view of the problems related to racial imbalance in both the suburbs and Rochester. Several of the more sensitive suburban superintendents invited Goldberg to visit their districts and make his presentation at either a closed session of the board or in an open board meeting. The superintendent agreed and accepted invitations from more than half the eighteen school districts in February 1965.

Although the presentation was basically identical in each district, the responses were different. Attendance at the public meetings varied from several hundred to well over a thousand. Closed sessions were limited to members of the board and upper echelon school personnel. The superintendent's contention that suburban participation would be a sterling form of enlightened self-interest met with mixed response. In some instances the public reaction was vitriolic and abusive; in others the meeting ended with the admonition, "Don't call us, we'll call you."

Public meetings received extensive coverage in both the city and suburban press. The most space regrettably was given to extremists, and the news media tended to characterize the sessions as conflicts between groups with fixed positions rather than as exploratory discussions designed to identify areas of common concern. The sessions did have a strong, positive influence though on urban-suburban relations. The most important by-product of the meetings was the creation of a new group. Dean Fullagar and the superintendents concluded there was great need for meetings which involved both city and suburban personnel. It was argued if the concern was expanded beyond that of racial imbalance, the solution of pressing fiscal and other problems might lead to the development of a milieu within which the issue of racial minorities could be discussed more dispassionately.

An informal group known as the Monroe County School Superintendents' Group was formed and met once a month at the Faculty Club of the University of Rochester. Creation of an agenda committee which included representatives from the city, the university, and the suburbs insured a comprehensive examination of current school issues. To insure wider involvement, the position of chairman was rotated.

All meetings were dinner meetings and thus provided an air of informality which was sorely needed. Meetings were closed, and the absence of the press was an important factor in determining the character and content of the discussion. At a later date the group decided to include the board president from each district and thus doubled the membership from nineteen to thirty-eight.

The enlarged group continues to meet regularly and the discussions have contributed to the growth of the program. There are now five suburban school districts directly involved in the transfer program. The original group of twenty-four pioneer transfer pupils from the inner city has now grown to 546. Despite the conflict precipitated by the original program in West Irondequoit, four other districts have followed the lead and one of these districts, Pittsford Central School District, now has a larger enrollment—130—of inner city pupils than Irondequoit—96. It is unlikely that these impressive gains would have been achieved if the Monroe County School Superintendents' Group had not been created.

It is important to note that the addition of board presidents served to pave the way for considerable unrestrained discussion of racial issues and ancillary problems. In some cases, the Board members were less timorous and more activist in the area of urban-suburban cooperation than were the administrators. Reluctant superintendents could no longer seek refuge in the contention that they had to "discuss this with the board." The presence of the board president helped to expedite decisions that would have been shelved pending approval by those legally responsible for the schools.

Today gradualism in any area of American society is categorically rejected by many activists. Rochester's efforts to solve the problem of imbalance have been viewed as successful by those who elect to contrast it with the modest results of programs in other sections of the nation. In some cases, however, activists are prone to describe our achievements as an extreme form of gradualism. Statistics can be interpreted to permit the conclusion that ours has been an *overwhelming* success or to support the inference that the numbers remain *relatively* small.

The first trans-urban exchange of students (Nov. 27, 1963) involved social studies classes from James Madison and John Marshall high schools. That summer (1964) the Brighton School District invited twenty-five inner city elementary pupils to attend summer school in Brighton. This was increased to thirty-five during the following summer, and the costs were shared by the P.T.A.'s in Brighton and in the sending inner city school.

West Irondequoit made the major breakthrough in September 1965 by its acceptance of twenty-four first grade pupils from #19 School. Brighton continued its support for a summer program and accepted forty-two pupils for summer 1966.

The Brockport Campus School, a part of the State University College at Brockport, organized a special summer session that involved 150 pupils of whom seventy-five were from Rochester's inner city and seventy-five from Brockport. Other school districts followed these examples, and the summer program was expanded greatly.

Success of the toe-wetting summer sessions was a major factor in the acceptance of school year exchanges, and by September 1966 West Irondequoit ceased to be the sole suburban school district with inner city pupils. Brighton accepted fifty-seven pupils from Rochester School #15, and The Harley School, a private country day school, awarded full scholarships to six pupils from the central city. Rochester School #20 completed arrangements to send thirty-two elementary pupils to the Brockport Campus School.

The summer school program reached its peak during summer 1968 when Brighton, Brockport, Penfield, Pittsford, Greece, and Webster accepted a total of 797 inner city pupils. Curtailment of this phase of the exchange program was forced by a sharp reduction in the availability of federal funds. The enrollment of inner city pupils in suburban districts for the school year continues to increase, however, but at a slower rate.

Suburban parochial schools entered the program in 1967 and accepted ninety-one inner city pupils. In view of the legal obstacles that prohibit assignment of public funds to parochial schools, their participation in the transfer program is especially noteworthy. It is significant that some of the parochial schools are located in suburban districts where public school authorities have refused to become involved in the transfer plan.

Evaluation

An analysis of achievement test data (1966-69) for inner city children who are attending schools in Irondequoit under the Urban-Suburban Transfer Plan showed that thirteen first grade pupils took the Metropolitan Achievement Test in 1966 and the average grade equivalent score was 1.9. Only three of the inner city children scored above 2.0, which is the normal grade equivalent for pupils who have completed first grade. When the same pupils were tested at the end of the second year, nine achieved above the grade equivalent. The average score was 3.3, which is significantly higher than expected level for that grade.

In spring 1969 the same thirteen pupils were given another Metropolitan reading test and the average grade equivalent was 4.04. Although the gains were not so impressive as those recorded during the previous year, the improvement trend did continue. Comparable data were compiled (1967-69) for a new group of sixteen first graders and the results were not noticeably different from the achievement gains made by the first group.

The data thus clearly indicate that inner city first graders who transferred to Irondequoit showed significant improvement in reading. Because of the transient nature of the population in inner city schools, a stable control group could not be identified. The results obtained in the transfer program, however, appear to be a complete reversal of the usual trend for reading achievement in inner city schools. Usually children who are near or below the grade equivalent at the end of the first grade are likely to fall farther behind at subsequent grade levels.

It is still too early for us to make final judgments as to the effectiveness of our programs with suburban schools, or to say which ones will prove most valuable. Patterns are beginning to emerge, however. We know, for instance, that Negro children transferring to Irondequoit and to Brighton have done better in their school work than a control group of children remaining at Rochester's School #19. There is clear indication that if we are to continue to move forward, we must do so on a metropolitan basis.

Project *Unique*: The World of Inquiry School

Among the many responses to the civil disorders which occurred in 1964 in Rochester was a planning conference called by city school officials to seek assistance from schools of education in the public and private colleges and universities of metropolitan Rochester. Urban educators are frequently disenchanted with the resources that are available in schools of education. School officials in Rochester were more fortunate. Dr. William A. Fullagar, Dean of the School of Education, University of Rochester, assigned Dr. Dean Corrigan to work full time with the superintendent and his staff to design programs which would seek solutions to the problems facing Rochester. Dr. Norman Kurland and personnel from the newly formed Center of Innovation, State Education Department, also participated in the initial planning.

A major step in the planning that culminated in Project UNIQUE was the conduct of the Community Resources Workshop during summer 1966. The participants were representatives of public and parochial schools and many segments of the urban community. Large and small group sessions were organized to encourage discussion and to develop a climate conducive to the sharing of ideas and free exchange of opinion. Out of these sessions came many proposed solutions for the problems of urban education. Members of the Project UNIQUE Planning Committee decided to design a new type of school rather than put all their hopes in an attempt to reclaim the old through compensatory programs of remediation.

The Project UNIQUE Planning Committee gave strong support to integration and redistribution of children to reflect a cross section of the population. Consideration was given to a variety of administrative devices including educational parks, open enrollment, two-way busing and other organization patterns. It was decided that where integrated schools existed every effort had to be exerted to maintain them. Where racial imbalance existed all available devices had to be utilized to dissolve it. But where racial imbalance could not be immediately corrected, all the resources of the larger community had to be brought to bear to assure equal educational achievement, even if this meant giving a disproportionate share of the resources to those schools that had large numbers of children with low achievement. The committee concluded that delay was an extravagant luxury and that comprehensive surveys and studies could no longer be substituted for results.

The apparent commitment of the community and the availability of funds resulted in the selection of a permanent planning staff. Ideas were solicited from parent-teacher groups, faculty meetings, educational conferences, church, civic, industrial, and civil rights groups. Attempts were made to assess community knowledge, interest, and feelings. Discussions and interviews were designed to create a community atmosphere that would accept and support quality, integrated education.

The completed proposal for Project UNIQUE was presented to the U. S. Office of Education in January 1967, and Federal approval was received in May. Three components were eliminated, nine were funded, and the Center for Cooperative Action in Urban Education was created to coordinate the entire project.

Project UNIQUE was created and implemented by people who were convinced that the ills of public education were neither inevitable nor beyond solution. They cited the need for a semi-autonomous unit that would be part of the Rochester City School District, but would be able to chart an independent course which could be altered in accordance with the changing needs of the community. Since it would not be burdened with the task of operating and maintaining traditional schools, UNIQUE would be free to explore new approaches to persistent problems.

World of Inquiry School

Part of the problem with urban education is the inequality of educational opportunity brought about by geographic, economic, and racial barriers. Stratification has proliferated to the point where the affluent are separated from the poor, white from black, and city from suburb. This stratification permits excellence to thrive in one part of the city while failure exists in another.

The World of Inquiry School, one of the nine components in Project UNIQUE, was designed as a geographic, ethnic, economic, racial, and academic composite of the student population in the metropolitan Rochester area. Pupils from all geographic areas of the central city, fringes of the city, and suburbs, attend the World of Inquiry School. As a result of a carefully planned selection process, 57 percent of the pupils are white, 36 percent Negro, 4 percent Puerto Rican, and 3 percent a mixture of other racial and ethnic groups. There is an equal distribution of boys and girls who range in age from three through eleven. The range in family income is from under $3,000 to over $40,000 per year.

To insure maximum academic and social achievement, the World of Inquiry School operates under a unique administrative structure, a more manageable pupil-teacher ratio, an innovative utilization of teaching and supportive staff, and maximum self-determination for its pupils. It also utilizes the talents of non-certificated, resource persons from the community as adjunct faculty. The school is non-graded and each pupil is permitted to progress at a rate comfortable for himself. Individualization of instruction and independent learning are possible because there is a copious supply of resources both human and material.

Pupils are grouped into "family units." The family unit is multi-aged, and thus more closely reflects a true family. To group children simply because they are the same age is artificial. This might be a minor concern, but the school is trying to martial all the pupil's resources in a concerted effort to increase achievement in a natural setting. In this environment children are encouraged to help each other and are themselves helped in the process. They learn to share and to be compassionate; to help someone else to learn induces the child to review and reinforce what he already knows about the material being discussed.

Teachers are cautious about making group assignments and the inquiry or discovery method is utilized extensively. Each child follows an individual curriculum designed specifically for him. The child, with the help of his teacher, makes his schedule. He decides where he wants to go and how long he wants to stay. He has a chance to satisfy his curiosity.

The instructional program is organized around the family rooms. There is a nursery unit with three-and four-year-olds, primary units with ages ranging from five through eight, and inter-mediate units for those eight through eleven. In addition to the family units there are interest centers in science, health and physical education, art, music, library and material resources, social studies, and industrial technology. Each center is staffed by a certificated and skilled teacher who is sometimes assisted by a teacher aide and highly competent resource persons from the community. The staff of an interest center is available to any child who wants to spend some time in the center.

Basic instruction in language arts and number skills occurs in the family room. The teacher individualizes instruction and keeps records of each pupil's progress in major subject areas. Preparation of a single lesson or assignment for use with the entire group is unlikely. Among major innovations which are being introduced is the use of "adjunct" faculty members who are talented, though non-certificated, teachers from the community. They are primarily used in interest areas with multi-aged and multi-ethnic groups with a wide range of ability. Children move throughout the school, from family room to interest areas and vice versa, both individually and in groups, to participate in a variety of activities.

Family room teachers are primarily responsible for individual and group pupil planning and guidance. The family room teacher and other staff members prescribe for the individual needs of the pupils. Parent conferences to discuss and evaluate individual pupil growth and progress are scheduled by the family room teacher, who arranges for involvement of the other specialists.

The school also has a Resource Associate in Intercultural Understanding. His primary function is to provide opportunity for human interaction which will improve racial attitudes on the part of whites and non-whites. He also provides opportunities for activities which will improve the student's personal feeling and self-image. The resource associate does this by working directly with children and by working with the staff. Positive racial attitudes are an established fact at the World of Inquiry School. On the questionnaires returned by parents, no one indicated anything but positive feelings toward integration.

The waiting list for pupils for the World of Inquiry School continues to grow and each addition can be considered a substantive endorsement of the major goal of Project UNIQUE—quality, integrated urban-suburban education. Although the school's "neighborhood" is metropolitan Rochester, the building is located in the inner city. The building itself is old, but internally it is new, and it houses an educational program that could be a prototype for the future. Standardized test scores reveal a spread along the entire range of achievement. The faculty spans a wide range of professional experience. Some had considerable experience prior to their assignment to the World of Inquiry School, others began their teaching careers there. Within this mass of contradictions, some promising educational methods are developing.

Responses to questionnaires mailed to parents in November revealed a high degree of pupil enthusiasm for the school program. The return on the first questionnaire was 94 percent, and almost all of the respondents (98 percent) indicated that their children go to school eagerly each day. For 51 percent of the children this reflected a change from their attitude the previous year. A follow-up questionnaire in February was returned by 91 percent and the responses were essentially the same.

Experimentation has not been restricted to the daily educational program. Parent involvement in the operation of the World of Inquiry School could conceivably be the model for an advisory committee that could be organized in every school district in Rochester. The primary concern of parents at the World of Inquiry School is quality, integrated education. Because of the diversity of its student body, parent involvement is a vital factor in the development of a feeling of belonging and in de-emphasizing the tendency to consider the school as something totally removed from one's neighborhood. The World of Inquiry School has proved that references to "our school" need not be limited to schools located within the immediate area of the home. In the same way that many colleges have succeeded in obtaining strong support from alumni throughout the state and nation, on a more modest scale the World of Inquiry School has succeeded in developing a strong sense of loyalty among those whom it serves.

An indication of the positive attitudes toward the school and education on the part of children and parents is the high percentage of parents who come to the school to act as tour guides, to observe classes, to attend special programs, and to assist in many ways. Many of them just want to be "a part of the excitement of the school" and appear frequently.

The school has demonstrated a method for raising the level of achievement of children within the inner city. It has also succeeded in bridging the gap between urban and suburban. These important educational and social accomplishments can be extended only if there is a climate within the educational structure which is receptive to change and if the public is willing to provide the resources necessary for implementation.

Opponents of metropolitan school districts have insisted for years that suburban parents would not send their children to an inner city school. There are presently over 500 suburban pupils on the waiting list for admission to the World of Inquiry School. It is important to note that neither the Rochester City School District nor the World of Inquiry School has ever solicited applications. Because of the pressure for admission, extensive publicity has been given to the size of the waiting list in an attempt to deter parents from filing applications.

Summary

Our experience proves that suburban parents, like inner city parents, want their children to attend the best school that is available. Location, busing, and racial composition of the student body are not automatically the determining factors. Participation in a two-way busing program between the city and the suburbs can be achieved when the quality of education is uniformly high in both areas. The World of Inquiry School is corroborative evidence that integrated education need not be achieved at the expense of quality education. The public must learn that these qualities are inter-related and must stop considering them as incompatible goals.

The City School District of Rochester has declared its commitment to the principle of quality, integrated education. We believe that attitudes which postpone or retard school integration can have no place in the future of American public education. Such attitudes are not healthy for children, who will live in a multi-racial, metropolitan society. It is essential that we do everything possible in education to assure our children have broad human contacts as they are growing to maturity. Society must recognize its basic responsibility for working to achieve the ideal of completely equal opportunities for all.

III

Project *Apex*: Magnet Schools for Enrichment and Exchange in Los Angeles

Albert W. Stembridge

Introduction

For the past four years, the Los Angeles City Unified School District has had the privilege of carrying out an exciting and innovative educational program—Project APEX, an acronym standing for Area Program for Enrichment Exchange.

Submitted as a proposal under the Elementary and Secondary Education Act of 1965, the project became the first in the district to receive a Title III grant ($426,200) in February 1967.

During the period between February and September 1967, Isaac H. McClelland, Superintendent of Secondary Area D, and Eugene Olson, Administrative Coordinator, involved community representatives, school district personnel, university personnel, private and parochial school educators, and students in comprehensive planning activities. At that time this writer participated as a secondary school principal, later becoming the director of the project in February 1969. Activities included numerous committees concentrating on curriculum development, student exchange schedules, equipment and supplies, textbooks, guidance and counseling programs, university participation, community involvement, and evaluation procedures.

Implementation of the program in four senior high schools began in September 1967. Full implementation was realized in February 1968, when a total of five senior high schools and eight junior high schools (ninth grade only) were included in the program.

Objectives of the Project

Project APEX features five major components which are designed to accomplish these objectives:
1) Provide specialized subject centers in many disciplines.
2) Offer an opportunity for students to study in an integrated atmosphere.
3) Provide a comprehensive guidance and counseling program through a single guidance center and special counselors at each APEX school.
4) Make use of the knowledge, resources, and facilities of a major university.
5) Involve the community and its resources in offering services and support programs.

Components of the Project

Subject Centers. Through its subject centers, APEX applies the university concept to secondary schools. In a university, a student enrolled in one college or school may take classes in other colleges or schools. Similarly, a student enrolled in one APEX school may take classes at another APEX school.

Educational enrichment is offered in five subject centers which have made available more than 90 courses—50 of which are new additions to the secondary curriculum.

University Involvement

The University of Southern California School of Education is an integral part of the APEX effort. Over the years scores of professors have presented lectures to APEX classes and conducted tours of the university facilities; APEX students have been frequent guests at sporting events; marine biology classes have enjoyed scientific excursions aboard the Valero IV laboratory ship; Saturday seminars and computer training workshops have been offered; full

TABLE 1

New Courses Developed by APEX or Offered
Through Voluntary Student Exchange

Aeronautics
Aeronautics Science 1, 2
Agriculture
Animal Technology   Man and His Environment
Floriculture   (Team teaching)
General Laboratory Animal   Plant Science
Horticulture(Co-ed) (Landscaping) Soil Science
Horticulture Mechanics   Vocational Laboratory
Art
Advanced Art Media   Photography
  Creative Arts in the Mass Media Studio 1 (Art Media)
Ceramics   Studio 2 (Printmaking)
Jewelry
Business Education
Computer Programming,   Data Processing, Keypunch 1, 2
  Introduction to   Exploratory Business Education
Data Processing, Introduction to Merchandising & Marketing
English
Advanced Placement English   Mass Media English
Afro Literature   Oral Interpretation of Literature
Creative Writing   Play Production
Linguistics   Power Reading
Foreign Language
Advanced Placement French   Italian 1, 2, 3, 4
Advanced Placement Spanish   Japanese 1, 2, 3, 4
Chinese 1, 2, 3, 4   Latin 1, 2, 3, 4
French 1, 2, 3, 4   Portuguese 1, 2, 3, 4
German 1, 2, 3, 4   Russian 1, 2, 3, 4
Hebrew 1, 2, 3, 4   Spanish 1, 2, 3, 4
Homemaking Education
Commercial Sewing   Home and Apparel Arts
Consumer Education   Nurse Aide
Diet Aide   Nursery Elementary Education
Health Occupations   Senior Home Economics
Mathematics
Advanced Algebra & Trigonometry Laboratory Mathematics
Advanced Placement Analytic   Computer Mathematics
  Geometry   Mathematics Analysis
Advanced Placement Calculus   SMSG Laboratory
Computer Laboratory Experience   Vector Geometry
Music
Comprehensive Musicianship   Harmony; Jazz Workshop
Concert Choir   Music History
Creative Problem Solving   Music Literature & Analysis
Science
Advanced Placement Chemistry   Enriched Physics; Marine Biology
Enriched Biology 1, 2   Microbiology-Bacteriology
Enriched Modern Science 1, 2   Special Research Seminar
Social Studies
Advanced Placement Amer. History Physical Geography
American Culture (Ethnic)   Psychology, Introduction to
Amer. Intercultural Heritage   Social Studies, Introduction to
Anthropology, Introduction to   Sociology, Introduction to
Asiatic Studies   Supreme Court & the Law
Latin Amer. Studies; Negro Hist. Urban Ecology and Demography
Specialty Subjects
Art-English-History (flexible   wood work, industrial crafts,
  schedule, team teaching)   power sewing, auto body & fender
Extended Work Experience   Lifetime Sports (Co-ed)
Health Occupations   Offset Printing
Industrial Occupation Classes: ROTC
  auto mechanics, drafting,   Telecommunications 1, 2, 3
  electronics, graphic arts,

privileges of the Doheny Library on the university campus have been accorded APEX students; and, courses on flexible scheduling and closed circuit telecommunications as well as other workshops for teachers and administrators have been conducted by university staff.

Community Involvement

The major sources of community involvement in APEX have been the Community Project for APEX, APEX Advisory Council, Voluntary Student Exchange Committee and the APEX Student Alumni Association.

Opportunities for community involvement were greatly enhanced in May 1967 when the Rosenberg Foundation funded the Community Project for APEX, sponsored by the Crenshaw Coordinating Council, the Exposition Coordinating Council, Crenshaw Neighbors, Inc., Crenshaw Youth Studies Association, and Neighbors Unlimited. Sharing a major concern in the area of urban education, these five sponsoring community groups saw Project APEX as a way to combat segregation and to help maintain a high quality of education in urban public schools.

Working as a team, the APEX director and Mrs. Joan Suter, Executive Director of the Community Project, conducted many tours of the project schools, appeared on panels at various meetings, made several radio and television programs, issued frequent news releases, and involved exchange students in numerous social and cultural events, including intergroup conferences on weekends.

Guidance and
Counseling Component

The APEX Guidance Center is located at Crenshaw High School and is under the direction of Mrs. Toni Walker, a secondary school counselor. Student activities include a variety of guidance and counseling services. In addition to individual counseling and group guidance, students and their parents are counseled on an extended-day and Saturday referral schedule. Students and parents may receive immediate counseling at the center or at a university clinic. Group counseling for students and teachers is also provided by specialists from the University of California at Los Angeles. Students receive assistance in their guidance classes, including career advisement resource speakers. Individual tutoring is available. An experimental program was developed in which computers matched student qualifications with college admission requirements.

Voluntary Student
Exchange Component

As one of the school district's major moves toward integration, student voluntary exchange is a key component of the project. The exchange component gives a student a chance to broaden himself, to break out of the confines of his local environment, to meet new people, to be exposed to new points of view and to make new friends among students of other racial, ethnic and cultural backgrounds. One important aspect of student exchange is that it is not limited to the classroom. Students meet for assemblies, club events, evening socials, conferences, seminars and other extracurricular activities.

During the program's operation from autumn 1967 through spring 1969, 3,056 students or twenty-five percent of those enrolled in subject center classes participated by being bussed. More than fifty percent of the 981 students who were enrolled in two summer sessions were exchange students who provided their own transportation. There were 702 students enrolled through voluntary exchange from the three predominantly black and two predominantly white high schools during the 1969-70 year.

From the beginning of the program the tendency of students has been to continue to enroll where the classes of their choice were offered, with apparently little regard to ethnicity. Seventy-five percent of the students went to the schools where eighty percent of the courses were offered.

Exchange activities have ranged from the highly structured to the informal. In addition to project-sponsored events, there were activities sponsored by the Community Project for APEX and other parent groups.

High among the list of exchange activities conducted recently was the involvement of students from Beverly Hills High School. Beverly Hills is a high status city with a separate school district. The black population is less than one percent. The overall minority population is less than ten percent. Students from Beverly Hills through their student human relations clubs became interested in APEX and started participating in its exchange activities. Encouraged by Associated Students for APEX, an all-student group, Beverly Hills students not only participated in workshops and conferences but also through their own efforts donated the receipts of a play ($1,010) for a conference.

Evaluation of the Program

Evaluation by the student participants is typified by a letter to the editor of the *Los Angeles Times,* the city's largest daily newspaper.

The writer said:

I was there and it was one of the most beautiful experiences of my life . . . it was fun and an exchange of ideas combined. There were discussions of current events, race, education, and parent problems which enlightened everybody to the problems of "the other half " and of themselves . . . it (APEX) enables students to take classes they ordinarily would be unable to take, and it increases the social realm of Los Angeles youth.

Another result of the participation by Beverly Hills High School students was their enrollment in APEX classes. Eight students enrolled in predominantly black schools, provided their own transportation, and traveled approximately twenty-five miles daily to attend classes. Out of this experience the Beverly Hills Board of Education approved a two-way student exchange of twenty-five students during the 1970-71 school year. Other districts also have expressed interest in similar exchange programs.

In his study of the voluntary student exchange component of APEX, Possemato reported that participating students, teachers and administrators give APEX a solidly positive endorsement. He noted that students praised the contents of the courses, the quality of instruction, and the variety of offerings. Exchange students were uniformly enthusiastic about their contacts with other ethnic school populations. Home school students were also positive, but at a somewhat lesser level. The shortcomings noted included the problems created by differing school schedules and the fact that the exchange, while integrating certain classes, was insufficient to assure fully integrated schools. In addition, some pupils lacked the background for highly academic courses.

Over the years students have volunteered many comments. The transportation and scheduling problem did receive some comments, but most were about the class, the instruction, and the exchange. Comments indicate that the students consider the exchange activities just as vital a part of the program as the instructional part.

A typical positive comment regarding attitudinal change is this made by a student in a formal presentation to the Los Angeles City Board of Education:

To me APEX is a giant step towards black and white understanding each other. APEX gives us the chance to feel each other's ghetto. When I say each other's ghetto, I mean our different surroundings. I was raised in a part of the city where white was not accepted. I was taught to hate the white until the seventh grade. From the seventh grade I began to explore about whites on my own. I couldn't do much exploring until APEX came along.

Before APEX came, I didn't know schools like Fairfax and Beverly Hills existed. When APEX came, I had the chance to feel and see how it was to go to an all white school. And for the first time, my friends weren't only black. APEX has given me a different concept of our racial problems. Who knows? APEX might be a start of a new trend—"Black and White together."

Parents of participants in project classes have also participated in the evaluation of the program. Parent comments primarily concerned the multicultural aspects of the program. A typical comment was as follows:

You have all heard of the academic values received from the APEX program, but what I think is even more important is the human relations aspect of the whole thing. As a parent whose child was involved in the interchange, I saw what an effect it had on her and her friends who were also in the program. The interchange and discovery of common problems hit most of the pupils very strongly. The realization of the fact that, basically, they were human beings though of different ethnic and religious backgrounds actually raised the dignity of each. Personally, I feel that the white child who went into a predominantly black school gained so much it is hard to put it in words. The warmth exchanged, the sharing of experience and the humanizing of many was fantastic. The realization by many black students that the white kids had as many "hang-ups" as they, if not more, was almost traumatic in its uplifting effect.

If this program did nothing else but make a few of our future leaders more cognizant of the fact that all people are first human beings, then I feel we have been a success.

Administrators rated the subject centers at their home schools and the exchange component. Ratings show a clear pattern. The subject centers are consistently rated "very effective" by their administrators, while the student exchange is rated as "effective." Comments differed significantly over the years. Originally administrators were concerned most about uniformity and specific details of the program. At the close of the second year their concerns were about the maturity of the students involved and their academic preparedness. Most recent ratings show that many were pleased with the positive reactions from parents and pupils about the quality of the program. Administrators have also shown a change to acceptance of a more "open" campus and fewer restrictions on pupil mobility and exchange activities.

Summary and Conclusion

Evaluation of the Area Program for Enrichment Exchange indicates that this pilot project has been a valuable and productive venture for the Los Angeles City Unified School District. In July 1970, upon the recommendation of Superintendent of Schools

Robert E. Kelly, the members of the Board of Education voted unanimously to restore the program with local funds after Title III funds terminated in June 1970.

Those involved with APEX believe that the project has yielded many benefits. It has shown a new direction for secondary education that can be followed in developing curriculum, planning instruction, using special materials and sophisticated hardware, involving staff and community, achieving cost effectiveness and, especially important, improving human relations and understanding. The APEX concept, moreover, is exportable to other school districts, and can be geared to elementary as well as secondary grade levels. Through the cluster complex, APEX has been a way in which vocational and college counseling can be provided to many students in several schools through a single guidance center.

The project has provided many opportunities for creativity on the part of teachers and administrators in the development and implementation of innovative programs. APEX has demonstrated how quality education and enrichment can be achieved in an integrated setting.

IV

Chicago's School Without Walls: The Chicago Public High School for Metropolitan Studies

Edgar G. Epps

Concepts and Goals

Metro, the Chicago Public High School for Metropolitan Studies, is an imaginative attempt to establish a "School Without Walls," patterned after Philadelphia's parkway program, Metro was planned by the Chicago Board of Education and the Urban Research Corporation (URC). This new type of high school is designed to offer students more and better instruction than traditionally organized schools at a lower per pupil cost. The planning document asserted that:

A school without walls multiplies the educational options available to the student and thus provides a much greater opportunity for the development of individual aptitudes and interests. It enables the students to participate in educational activities that are related to their personal and vocational goals, thus increasing the likelihood that they will learn and apply basic skills that may not seem relevant when taught in the isolation of the classroom.

Metro is not so much a revolt against the typical goals of American education as it is an assault on the educational practices that are perceived as barriers to the attainment of these goals. Metro High School, in fact, was designed to implement some of the gen-

erally accepted goals of American education. The goals emphasized in planning the Metro Program included the following:
1) The mastery of those skills needed to function competently in our rapidly changing society.
2) The growth of self-esteem and independence of thought and action based upon the development of the student's aptitudes and interests.
3) The capacity to relate interpersonally with people from diverse backgrounds and interests.
4) An understanding of societal processes and pressing social problems.

The Metro program was planned on the assumption that these goals could be achieved most effectively through several fundamental concepts in organization and instruction. The concepts emphasized in designing the school and its program include: 1) use of existing business and institutional facilities instead of a separate school plant; 2) enrollment of students from all sections of the city of Chicago, representing the total academic, geographic, racial, and economic diversity of high school youth; 3) reduction of rigid classifications of students into vocational and academic groupings; 4) development of flexible curricular offerings, and 5) participation of students, teachers, parents and administrators in decision making.

In spite of the substantial amount of innovation involved in the Metro program, Metro graduates are expected to meet the requirements established for high school education by the Chicago Board of Education, the Illinois School Code, and the North Central Association. Graduates of the program will receive the standard high school diploma from the Board of Education. Metro's principal expects more than half the students to enter college after graduation.

Instructional Program

Metro High School is now located on the second, third, and fourth floors of a building on Dearborn Street in downtown Chicago. The Metro student body of 350 students is divided into two groups or centers. One center is composed of ninety freshmen and sixty sophomores and juniors who entered Metro for the first time in autumn 1970. This center is located on the second floor. The other center is based on the fourth floor of the building (the central offices are on the third floor). The fourth floor center is composed of 150 returning students and fifty new freshmen. The purpose of having two centers is to make it possible for a strong sense of community to develop in each of the two groups.

The Metro curriculum offers students a number of approaches to learning basic skills, mastering subject content, and developing positive personal characteristics. The program uses the resources of its staff and of businesses, cultural institutions, and community organizations to provide learning experiences that have vitality and rigorous yet individualized standards. The curriculum is organized into Units, Counseling Groups, and Core Courses.

Units are learning experiences that are complete within themselves. Some are taught by the Metro staff and some are taught by people from participating businesses, cultural institutions, and community groups. Units are organized so that they fit into one or more discipline areas such as English, mathematics, science, social studies, and foreign language. Specific Metro learning units, such as TV Production, Principles of Electricity, Modern European Art, Singing for Fun, and Mathematics Laboratory, range from highly practical to extremely creative and some might be considered esoteric. Each student signs up for approximately four units during each learning cycle. The academic year is divided into four nine-week learning cycles.

Counseling Groups meet every Wednesday afternoon. Each student is assigned to a counseling group in his Center. The general purpose of the counseling group is to provide a place for the student to discuss his overall progress and educational goals in a group, to work with one staff member in making decisions about his educational program, and to provide an opportunity for him to get to know other Metro students through discussions, picnics, trips, and other activities. Counseling groups, at the end of the first learning cycle, were found to be the most effective forum within the school in which to discuss school problems.

Core Courses provide students with in-depth educational experiences planned and taught cooperatively by groups of teachers. Each core course is taught by three teachers and focuses on a particular problem or broad area of study (neighborhoods, communications, pollution, etc.). The core course approaches a problem or area of study through a variety of disciplines. A core course dealing with pollution, for example, might involve writing a pamphlet or preparing a film about pollution and the law enforcement activities in this area (social studies), and analyzing the effects of chemical pollution on animals (science). Each student receives English and social studies credit for his work in the core course. He also must choose an additional subject area on which he wants to focus as part of the core course. He also receives credit in that area.

The Metro program allows a student to pursue his own interests and develop the abilities he decides are important while still fulfilling the four-year requirements for high school graduation. Each core course and unit is assigned a certain number of credits. A Metro student fulfills graduation requirements through a combination of work in units and core courses. A freshman student, for example, would normally take English, social studies, mathematics or science, another major subject, physical education, and perhaps art. He could receive half of his English, social studies, and science credit through the core course, and the balance through units in these areas. He would also fulfill credit in an additional major subject, in physical education, and in art through unit work.

Units and courses at Metro are not organized on an "ability group" or grade level basis. Students select their courses and organize their educational program in consultation with teachers and counselors. Student interests and needs determine the content of the program. A recent report stated the following principle:

Students also participate actively in the evaluation process. Students are graded on a credit/no credit basis; letter grades are not used. The decision whether or not to award credit for a unit is reached as a result of a discussion between the student and teacher concerning the student's progress in the unit. Active participation in evaluation encourages students to develop a sense of responsibility with respect to their own educational progress.

Implementation

Facilities

One way to insure that learning takes place in a variety of settings is to operate a school without a conventional school building. In February 1970, Metro High School opened for business in offices located on the fifteenth floor of an office building on State Street in the heart of Chicago's loop. Classroom space was provided by more than forty businesses, museums, art galleries, and community organizations. During its opening learning cycle, students were provided opportunities for studying astronomy at Adler Planetarium, anatomy in a university anatomy department, mathematics on another university campus, film making at the public library or a television station, and electronics at the telephone company. This pattern of using the city and its institutions as Metro's campus is an integral part of the school's philosophy.

The experience gained during Metro's first cycle of operation resulted in an awareness on the part of the staff and Urban Research Corporation consultants that a well designed meeting place was highly important. A basic characteristic of the program that makes it work is a sense of community, binding together students and staff who are involved in diverse activities over a wide geographic area. Much of this sense of community is attributable to Metro's small size (150 students during its first cycle of operation; approximately 350 students during the 1970-71 school year). To take advantage of the opportunity to build a sense of community, adequate central office space is needed to facilitate open communication of information about schedule changes, special events, and other matters of general concern to students and staff. Space in the central facility should also provide opportunities for independent reading and special projects.

One of the early problems encountered by Metro concerned its location in a commercial office building. Other occupants of the building complained about student behavior on elevators and in halls. The problem was alleviated by the students themselves setting a norm for behavior.

After the first learning cycle of operation, Metro moved its headquarters to a new location. The features sought in the new facility included location in the heart of the downtown business district, access to public transportation, and availability of space near enough to the ground so that students could use the stairs for entering and leaving the central office (thereby avoiding the elevator problems encountered in the original facility). Important considerations taken into account in planning for the use of the new central office space included room for office clerical work, quiet space for study, space for two and three person conferences, seminar rooms, space for individual and small group project work, and space for relaxation.

In order to maintain the sense of community established during the first learning cycle, Metro students and staff decided that no status distinctions should dictate the use of space. Students who want to have conferences use the same space as faculty members who want to hold conferences. Although the new offices are located on three floors of the building, this does not seem to have lessened the sense of community that characterizes the program.

Metro experienced problems with its central office space again in 1971. This time a circuit judge ordered the school board to vacate the building because a Fire Department complaint found the building in violation of city building code specifications. The owners of the building subsequently renovated it to comply with city building codes, but Metro was forced to seek alternative operating space for four weeks while the repairs were being made. Tom Wilson, Urban Research Corporation Consultant working with Metro, reported in a recent conversation that support from the community enabled Metro to continue operations with only one day of interruption. Space was donated by many businesses and organizations for classes and other activities. Strong support also came from the school board, the superintendent of schools, local newspapers and the parents. In fact, it is reported that this problem resulted in the most effective parent participation since the beginning of the program. Students, faculty, administrators, parents, and community leaders all joined in the effort to keep the school in operation until the space problem could be solved.

The reader may wonder why so much attention is devoted to space problems in a short essay on Metro. The reason for this emphasis is to make persons who consider duplicating the "school without walls" aware of the vital importance of central office space. Not just any old building will do. It must be centrally located, accessible to public transportation, and large enough to provide opportunities for enough activities to promote a sense of community. Consideration should also be given to whether or not students can use the stairs to enter and leave. Finally, the compatibility of the other tenants and the diversified teenage population must be considered.

Informality

Metro's sense of community is also encouraged by the air of informality that characterizes the relationships between staff and students. The Principal, Nathaniel Blackman, is called "Nate" by the students; office and teaching staff are also called by their first names. Students, therefore, feel that the principal and the teachers are approachable and accessible. The principal calls all-school meetings to discuss problems such as class cutting or complaints from the building management. After open discussion of these problems, students and staff reach decisions about appropriate behavior, procedures, or standards. According to the staff, the combination of student participation in decision making and an absence of petty regulations has resulted in a school with few problems of discipline or student dissent.

Student Selection

The Metro student body was selected in a manner to insure diversity. The 110 ninth graders in the initial class were selected by lottery from among 1000 applicants. The forty juniors and seniors were selected in accordance with the principle of diversity, but leadership qualities were included among the selection criteria for the upper-classmen. Two males and two females were selected from each high school, thus assuring that the sexes were equally represented and that the student body reflected the racial and social class distribution of the city's high school population. The student body is approximately 54 per cent black. Random selection procedures were also used to select the 200 new students who entered Metro in September 1970 (140 ninth graders, forty tenth graders, and twenty eleventh graders). Applications to Metro exceed available slots by at least ten to one.

In spite of the great diversity which characterizes the Metro student body, there is a friendly atmosphere at the school. Students report that Metro is more humane and personal than their previous schools. Race relations are also congenial. There is an absence of conflict, and tensions are minimal. The pricipal reported that there were no fights among the students and that there was little stealing or vandalism.

Teacher Selection

Metro's teachers, iike the students, are representative of the city-wide racial distribution of public school teachers; currently they are two-thirds white. They differ from the typical teacher in several important respects. First of all, and perhaps most importantly, they are volunteers. Applications for the 1970-71 school year exceeded the number of positions available by a ratio of ten to one. The procedures used in the selection of teachers for the 1970-71 school year are described in the report on Metro's first learning cycle. Applications were first forwarded to the personnel department of the Board of Education. The applications of qualified applicants were then forwarded to Metro. Applicants were requested to fill out a questionnaire designed to provide information directly relevant to the special demands of the Metro program. A standing committee appointed by the principal and consisting of students, staff, and Urban Research Corporation personnel reviewed each application. The standing committee was divided into interview and review sub-committees, each composed of one Metro student, one Metro staff member, and one URC staff member. In the process, each subcommittee recommended to the principal that an applicant be classified for immediate consideration, future consideration, or no further consideration. Applicants classified for immediate consideration were requested to appear at Metro for an interview. These interviews were conducted with a group of three to four candidates by an interviewing subcommittee formed as described above. Twenty-seven applicants were recommended by the committee for immediate consideration. The principal then made staff selections from this list.

Metro's teachers are a relatively young group; most teachers are in their twenties or thirties. I asked Mr. Blackman what qualities he looked for when selecting teachers. First on his list of teacher characteristics was "ability to relate to others." This is a necessity in a school which attempts to foster close interpersonal relationships among all members of the staff and student body. Other attitudes considered important included "the ability to recognize individual differences, ability to accept change, and willingness to work long hours (dedication).

One other characteristic mentioned by Mr. Blackman was patience. He elaborated on this point by stating that the Metro program was "not initially designed for black students." It takes time and patience to learn to deal with black students' problems. The kind of problems discussed by Mr. Blackman focused on changing the students' sense of responsibility with respect to their educational programs. One of the basic goals of the Metro program is to help students assume responsibility for directing their own education. This requires that students learn to assert themselves, to speak out in group discussions, and to tell teachers what they are doing that is wrong or right.

Patience is also demanded of teachers as they struggle to decide which aspects of black culture and/or youth culture should be encouraged, ignored, or discouraged. Black teachers, according to Mr. Blackman, appear to encounter fewer tensions in dealing with these problems. There is a tendency for some white teachers in this situation to be too accepting; some teachers are reluctant to set any kind of behavioral standards for fear of being considered racist. Black teachers tend to find it easier to point out habits or behavior patterns which may be harmful to the black student or to the community and to make suggestions about potential modifications in behavior.

Plans for Evaluation

One of the most unique aspects of the Metro program is the interaction between Metro and the Urban Research Corporation (URC). URC's education division designed the program under a contract from the Chicago Board of Education, participated in the selection of the principal and staff, and has played an active part in every phase of the operation since its inception. The closeness of the relationship is supported by the location of URC staff offices in Metro's central office space. The URC team, supported by a research grant from the Urban Education Research Fund of the University of Illinois - Chicago Circle, has also been responsible for an extensive research and evaluation effort concerning the process of establishing Metro and the effects of the Program on participants.

The evaluation is designed to answer the following types of questions: What approaches are working in counseling? What problems are arising with participating organizations? What are the characteristics of an effective and amicable integrated situation? Which students are not being reached by the program and why?

The research and evaluation effort at Metro has two parts:

1) A long-term comparison of 110 Metro students randomly selected to attend Metro, and 110 control students still attending traditional schools. Intensive case studies of 16 students in each group are also being conducted.

2) A short-term evaluation the purpose of which is to clarify issues of immediate interest to program participants to aid them in planning and decision-making.

The evaluation instruments will include achievement tests and attitude measures such as indices of *sense of control and autonomy, self-image, aspirations and interests, interpersonal relations,* and *attitudes toward school.* The case studies will involve intensive interviews. It is hoped that the collection of pre- and post-test data on the experimental and control groups, and the interview data will enable the research team to provide interested educators with some rather definitive answers to questions about the effectiveness of the Metro Program. The URC team plans to use the Metro experience as a case study from which a model will be developed for providing technical assitance to other school systems in setting up similar alternative schools. The completion of data analysis is planned for the 1971-72 school year.

Preliminary reports indicate that Metro is already successful in some important respects. There is tentative evidence that academic achievement of Metro students surpasses that of students in the city as a whole. This may be attributable to halo effects or to selection effects, but it is encouraging. Students report they are enjoying school in a way they had never thought possible. Teachers and staff are enthusiastic about the creative possibilities involved in the Metro program.

In spite of this almost universal enthusiasm, Principal Blackman and URC consultants readily admit that Metro is not for everybody. "Some students cannot operate without the support of a structured environment." For this type of student, Metro is not the answer. The same is true for teachers who require a highly structured classroom or curriculum. There have been a few dropouts from the Metro program who have returned to their previous schools. The staff feels that this is as it should be. Metro students should feel they are in an educational environment which fits their personal needs. If the school does not meet the student's needs, he is permitted to return to his former school.

There are obviously some problems associated with the Metro type school. Conflict with business personnel in the office building have been mentioned. A few incidents have been reported of misunderstandings between Metro students and participating organizations. These have usually been resolved through discussions with staff, students, and participating organization personnel. Minor difficulties involving the use of public transportation by school age youngsters during the school day had to be resolved; policemen had to learn that Metro students were not truants. Problems of this type can be anticipated by other systems that attempt to establish a "school without walls."

Summary

During the past two years, the Urban Research Corporation, in cooperation with the Chicago Board of Education, has planned and assisted in the development of Metro High School. They have, with the involvement of staff and students, attempted to test and develop the following ideas about learning:

1) The possibilities for meaningful education are enhanced when such education occurs in real-life situations, including the businesses, cultural institutions, and neighborhoods of a city.
2) Students can learn from people with varied skills and interests— lawyers, electricians, artists, newspaper reporters. A skilled teacher can help the student use the talents of these people to gain a rich and individualized education.
3) A more human relationship between teacher and student fosters productive learning.
4) An urban school must be developed with student involvement in decision-making. Students become more independent and motivated learners by helping to make decisions about how their schools will be structured and how their own education will proceed.
5) A fairly small learning community of teachers and students (with no more than 200 participants) must be the basic unit to which the student relates. This community of learners must provide both constant support and constant evaluative feedback to the student regarding his directions for learning.
6) The diverse backgrounds of students provide a resource for education that should become an integral part of a school program.

While it is too early to declare Metro an unqualified success, it can be stated that the program has generated considerable support and enthusiasm among its students and in the city as a whole. Applications from new students continue to outstrip spaces available by more than ten to one, and applications from teachers have increased. All of this suggests that there is a demand for expansion of the program even before the evaluation has been completed. Discussion of additional centers has been undertaken by the consultants and the school board.

If we ask ourselves what makes Metro work, the evidence at hand seems to suggest that four factors are operative. They may be summarized as follows: 1) the fact that staff and students are selected from groups of volunteers predisposes them to react positively to the program; 2) the experimental nature of the program and the enthusiasm of the staff and consultants facilitate a halo effect; 3) individualization of instruction and student participation in decision making enhance the student's sense of adequacy and self-image, and 4) the small size of the student body facilitates group cohesiveness. While the designers of the program emphasize the importance of the "school without walls" aspect, much of the value of the Metro program probably could be achieved in a typical school building if the other ingredients were present.

Note

In preparing this essay, I have relied heavily upon reports prepared by members of the Educational Division of the Urban Research Corporation. I am deeply indebted to Messrs. Thomas A. Wilson, Richard Johnson, and Donald R. Moore for sharing these materials with me. I am also indebted to the above individuals and to Principal Nathaniel Blackman for granting me time for interviews.

V

Intergroup Relationships in a School Camp Environment

Denver C. Fox

"I don't want to go up in the mountains to live with no whities! You gotta live with 'em, sleep with 'em, and eat with 'em for a whole week."

"I will not have my child go to camp to live with blacks. He doesn't need this kind of experience. We are not racists. We have never had any problems with them. Why stir up trouble? Why don't you schedule our school to go to camp with children of our neighboring schools who have similar backgrounds and interests. You're just asking for trouble."

Here are expressions of two extreme points of view. The first comes from a black child in a school that has a majority of black and brown children. The second is the statement of a parent of a white child in a school with very few black children. While these attitudes are not necessarily typical either of black or white families, they symbolize some of the real problems which have been faced by educational leaders in San Diego City and County during a span of twenty-five years of school camping.

The Outdoor Education Program

The Outdoor Education Program for San Diego City and County was developed as a community effort which brought together representatives from the two governments, PTA's, school districts, service clubs, recreation departments, conservation groups, parents, state parks, the United States Forest Service, clubs, and a host of related groups and agencies. Responsibility for the development of program and policies rests with an Outdoor Educational Advisory Committee representing all school districts in the county and the San Diego City-County Camp Commission.(1) The responsibility for administering the program rests with a camp principal. The professional staff consists of four administrators, thirty-one camp teachers, seven teachers' aides, and three camp counselors. Administrators, teachers, and teachers' aides are employed by the San Diego City Schools and the La Mesa-Spring Valley School District. The camp counselors are employed by the San Diego City-County Camp Commission.

Cost of operation for the school camp, including accident insurance, clerical services, food, health, transportation, and utilities, is borne by parents of children who attend the camp. The cost of school camp instruction (teachers' salaries, instructional materials, and supplies) is borne by the fourteen participating school districts. Funds for buildings and capital equipment are provided by San Diego City and San Diego County, with the San Diego City-County Camp Commission having responsibility for administering these funds. Week-end and summer camp operations are financed by campers themselves or sponsoring organizations.

The San Diego experience in school camping began at Camp Cuyamaca in 1946. Since that time, the outdoor education movement has grown from one camp serving 1,000 sixth grade students annually to three camps serving more than 19,000 children coming from twenty school districts within San Diego County. During this quarter of a century of experience, the evolution and development of intercultural relationships in a camp environment has proved to be a significant aspect of the camp program. In order to understand the significance of intergroup relationships in a school camp operation it is useful to take a close look at the school camp program.

The Camping Program

Each Monday throughout the school year more than 550 sixth grade boys and girls go with their classroom teachers to the high mountains of San Diego County. Under the leadership of especially trained camp teachers they explore their new physical and social environments in what can be a thrilling and adventuresome learning experience. For five school days they live together in a camp and outdoor setting. They take an active part in planning their week, setting standards of behavior, and accepting the responsibilities that are a natural part of camping and outdoor living. The children grow in self-reliance and independence as they learn new skills by taking care of themselves.

The outdoor curriculum of the school camp program is a curriculum of action—working, exploring, discovering, creating, conserving, sharing, investigating, evaluating. The outdoor classroom includes many interesting places and things to study—hills, valleys, the river, the heavens, plants, and animals. The tools are the simple tools of the woodsman and craftsman—knives, axes, shovels, saws, files, chisels, hammers, drills, glue and sandpaper. The skills are those of the scientist—exploring, discovering, collecting, recognizing problems, planning, cooperating, proposing, testing, investigating, evaluating. The activities include studies in astronomy, geology, ecology, fire fighting, hiking, conserving soil, improving the forest, building dams, constructing bridges, planting trees, tracking animals, preparing and cooking meals over the open fire, tobogganing, sharing experiences around the campfire, carving in rock and wood, and singing and dancing.

The school camp provides a unique opportunity for the promotion of improved relationships among children. Cooperation and consideration for others become the means of gaining greater rewards from camp activities. The friendly, relaxed atmosphere of the outdoors provides a climate in which new friendships are made and increased understanding and respect for others can be developed.

Intergroup Relationships in the Camp Program

For the first twenty years of operation, from 1946 to 1966, there was little attempt to provide special treatment for children of minority groups. The approach to the school camp program during this period was to make every effort to minimize differences and treat all children alike. There was little racial friction in the informal climate of the camp environment.

As time passed, however, tensions in the adult world were increasingly reflected in the school camp program. The black community was crying out for justice and fair treatment and the white majority was confused and hurt by demands that threatened their comfortable world. By 1965, some of the integrated encampments were marked by problems in the relationships between black and white children.

Up to this time the camp program had sought simply to provide an experience in which children coming from different schools, different economic levels, and varied social, racial, and cultural groups could gain increased understanding and appreciation of each other. No efforts had been made to make special arrangements in scheduling so as to take into account race, culture, or economic status. This unstructured approach to scheduling sometimes resulted in a schedule that brought together schools with high proportions of black children. In addition, some aspects of the camping program were not contributing effectively to the goal of bringing about increased contact and better understanding among students of different backgrounds. It became apparent that the school camp program for 1966-67 would need to explore alternatives for improving intergroup relationships. The staff accepted this challenge in the belief that careful planning and initiative could do much to advance the goal. Since 1966-67, accordingly, a number of steps such as the following have been taken to improve intergroup relationships in the San Diego Camping Program:

1) Scheduling of schools to insure a good mix of children with varying backgrounds, cultures, and needs.
2) Structuring the cabin living situation to foster new friendships by assigning bunks so that each child has a familiar friend on one side and a previously-unknown bunk-mate on the other.
3) Providing for good social mix at the dining table by having children from each school at each table.
4) Encouraging intergroup contacts in camp activities by limiting the number of campers from each "sign up" group in a given activity and by having children sign up for interest groups without knowing the selections of their close friends.
5) Increasing staff effectiveness in promoting good intergroup relationships by giving more attention at staff meetings to planning and evaluating the human relationship aspects of the program.

In general, the efforts to strengthen the intergroup aspect of the camp program in 1966-67 were successful. There were, nevertheless, instances of hostility, aloofness, and feelings of superiority, although these tended to occur early in the week encampment and to diminish as the week progressed. But problems in intergroup relationships continued to become more acute in the camp, as indeed was the case in the adult community in San Diego County as well as elsewhere in the country. Among the factors which appeared to be responsible for a growing apprehension among campers and parents were 1) an increased sensitivity to the community problem of integration, with the accompanying increase in militancy, defensiveness, and fearful anticipation; 2) an increased number of campers whose background had not prepared them to take on the responsibilities as well as the opportunities of a camp experience; 3) the occasional absence of classroom teachers whose pupils were at camp, and 4) inaccurate reporting of incidents at camp by children who left early in the week taking with them alarming tales that had no basis in fact.

In order better to prepare children for the camp experience a set of suggestions was mailed to each participating teacher three weeks before his pupils were to go to camp in the 1967-68 season. Particular emphasis was given to ways in which the children could become acquainted with other schools participating in the camp session they would attend. Visits to schools were encouraged, as was letter writing between sixth grade students in the schools sending pupils to the same encampment. Students in the "advantaged" schools were encouraged to participate in money-raising projects to help finance camp scholarships for needy students. Teachers were urged to be at camp to help their students work out solutions to camp problems and to help them, in post-camp discussion, interpret and understand reasons for the problems encountered. Teachers were further reminded that a week of integrated living at camp would not be a panacea for the deep problems of intergroup relationships. They were urged to remind their students that the encampment was not a failure because problem situations occurred there, but rather that a problem situation provided an opportunity for a valuable learning experience in seeking an intelligent solution.

Implementation of proposals for improving intergroup relations in the school camp program resulted in marked progress in relationships among blacks and whites. But a new cry was being heard from Chicano groups, Americans of Mexican descent. The grievances and demands of the Chicano adults echoed those of the blacks. A new note of militancy had been added, followed by still another cry from the Indians who are native to the San Diego area. But the adaptations of programs which had been made for the blacks have proved sound enough to apply also to the Chicanos and Indians in the program. Efforts are being made to recruit Chicano and Indian as well as black teachers and aides for the program. A new type of position is being tailored to attract people who are not certificated, but who are otherwise competent to lead children in some of the many aspects of school camping.

A Look Ahead

The support that San Diego City and County give to their school camping and outdoor education program can be seen in their joint financing of new buildings and facilities to replace the old CCC buildings at Camp Cuyamaca and Camp Palomar. Reservations for the camping season of 1971-72 total 19,200, and continue the trend of annual increase in the number of campers served. The enterprise has developed primarily from local efforts. Continuing support of the San Diego city and county governments has been demonstrated in their joint financing in new buildings and facilities costing $1,300,000.

The future of outdoor education and school camping in San Diego is now in the hands of many people who have participated in the program when they were in the sixth grade. The goodwill generated by a quarter of a million ex-campers over the past twenty-five years continues to provide support for the school camp program. As it should be, the future of school camping and outdoor education in San Diego will, in large part, be determined by the people who know it best.

Note

(1) The San Diego City-County Camp Commission is made up of a city councilman, the county supervisor, the superintendent of the city schools, the county superintendent of schools, the representative from the Ninth District, and a P.T.A. representative from the County Council.

VI

A Learning Center in an Integrated Elementary School

Erwin Pollack

Background of the Project

The Ray Independent Learning Center is a federally funded, three-year project at the Ray Elementary School in Chicago. The school is a K-8, seventy-five-year-old plant. It is located one block from the University of Chicago in the integrated, largely middle-class community of Hyde Park. Ray is one of only four fully integrated schools in Chicago with at least a substantial minority of middle-class children. It has a heterogeneous student body drawn from the university community and from low-income areas in Hyde Park and in the neighboring community of Woodlawn.

Chicago is the most segregated large city in the United States. Approximately seventy percent of its black population lives in contiguous neighborhoods that are ninety percent or more black. Twenty eight percent live in neighborhoods that are becoming all black and only two percent live in stable, predominantly white neighborhoods. But at Ray school the racial composition of the student body (40 percent white, 55 percent black, 5 percent Puerto Rican and other) since 1967 has approximated that of the public elementary school population of the city as a whole. Ray was a natural laboratory for a project with the prime objective of increasing individualized instruction and independent learning, while ensuring maximum interaction between races and classes and improving the quality of education in order to attract and retain middle-class families.

The idea for the Independent Learning Center grew out of discussions and efforts to meet the educational needs of the very different kinds of children who attend Ray. If the school were organized strictly according to academic achievement, the Woodlawn children would be set apart in the isolation which has already been a factor in their inability to do as well in school as the Hyde Park children. The school was organized in this way before 1965, and parents had been divided into factions pitting those who opposed the resulting *de facto* segregation against those who defended it. In 1963-64, Ray underwent a serious crisis when an *ad hoc* parents' group publicly challenged the practice of achievement grouping, and the resulting intra-school segregation. Before the crisis was over, almost every parent in the school had chosen sides. An effort to move away from achievement grouping at that time was unsuccessful.

In autumn 1965, the school got a new principal who was black. After two years of careful preparation with teachers and parents, as well as an intensive statistical analysis of achievement scores of all children in the school, the new principal instituted a program of planned heterogeneous grouping, with re-grouping for language arts and mathematics within each grade level in grades five through eight. Each class, then, except for language arts and mathematics, had a range of students from those below grade level to those well above grade level. The school, then, was no longer divided into two groups—one mostly white and achieving well, and one mostly black and lagging academically. The new arrangements won broad acceptance among teachers, students, and parents, but they also increased awareness of the need for additional measures and resources to serve the individual requirements of the children.

Although half the black children in Ray School in 1967 were from middle-class families, the loss of white children was continuing and the number of disadvantaged black children in the school was increasing. The pupils in kindergarten through fourth grade, approximately one-third of whom were black, came from that part of the community immediately adjoining the university. At the fifth grade level and again at the seventh grade level children entered the school from the adjoining Woodlawn community under a plan required by the Board of Education. Thus, with children from Woodlawn, the fifth and sixth grades were sixty-two percent black and the seventh and eighth grades were seventy-nine percent black. The problems of the school arose primarily from the extreme range of class, culture, and achievement levels.

Late in 1967, the Chicago school system was putting finishing touches on an elaborate plan to improve Woodlawn schools, but Ray school was outside the official Woodlawn boundaries. No special plan had been devised for Ray even though twenty-five percent of its students came from Woodlawn. The Ray PTA decided to force action, announcing it would appeal to universities to step in and give the help that the school system had withheld.

The parents got fast action. The associate superintendent of schools asked the principal to prepare a proposal for a grant under Title III of the Elementary and Secondary Education Act. The principal and several parents wrote a proposal for an Independent Learning Center to serve Ray's highly diverse student body. The proposal was approved by the United States Office of Education and a three-year grant was made.

Some of the most important functions of the Learning Center as stated in the proposal were as follows:

1) To support efforts of teachers toward increased individualization of instruction.
2) To establish a collection of materials on Afro-American history and culture.
3) To establish a collection of manipulative, tactile, and construction materials and of games relating to the learning of mathematical concepts.
4) To provide the school with a wider repertory of possible responses to the interests of the child as perceived and communicated by the parent.
5) To work with community organizations in relating the school to the on-going life of the community.
6) To seek involvement of special interest groups such as drama, art, and journalism, in a meaningful way in the school program.
7) To provide opportunities for meaningful interaction between children of different backgrounds.
8) To provide information to the community and to the Chicago public school system that would be of significant value in designing educational programs for other integrated schools and eventually for education parks.

How the Learning Center Operates

The Center is staffed by a director, two experienced teachers, a secretary and a research assistant. Use is also made of volunteers who come regularly to the Center to work with individual students or small groups. The Center is equipped with modern audio-visual aids (film loop projectors, tape recorders, a language master, filmstrip projectors, overhead projectors, slide projectors) a variety of self-instructional materials, word and number games as well as traditional games such as chess, checkers, and monopoly, and basic reference works. The Center is free to use its funds to obtain materials believed to be useful to students without having to observe constraints imposed by lists of "approved" materials. The Board of Education has installed a data processing unit in the Learning Center which includes two key punches and a computer terminal, one of only three such units in the elementary schools of the city.

During the first year of the Center's operation students from grades three through eight came to the Center upon recommendation of their teachers. They came for individual work in enrichment activities, remedial programs, and independent study. The Learning Center staff consulted with classroom teachers and received students referred by them for purposes determined by the teacher. Some teachers, especially sensitive to the needs of their students, recommended pupils for advanced or remedial work or perhaps just for some time in an unpressured setting. With its facilities and low teacher-pupil ratio the Center was able to work with individual children for a substantial period of time, something that teachers with large classes found difficult to do. Some 200 students were served in this way during the first year, oftentimes as many as thirty-five per period. Those recommended for help with a particular skill often stayed as long as they wanted, provided the staff believed their experiences were having a positive effect. Some were scheduled for one period daily, others for three or four periods per week, and others every day of the week. The schedules for individual pupils were determined by the director and the classroom teacher. Students kept records of their activities and maintained their own individual record folders. They evaluated their own progress on a weekly basis, and this record, together with the evaluation of the Learning Center staff, provided a progress report to be sent back to the recommending teacher.

During the first year we worked with selected pupils in many subjects, using a broad range of materials and equipment and a variety of resource people, consultants, and volunteers in an open, relaxed atmosphere. Pupils worked on black history, mathematics, spelling, high-interest readers, and how-to-study materials. The children made extensive use of the Center's equipment. They were given initial training by the staff and, upon acquiring the ability to operate the equipment effectively, they were encouraged to make wide use of it.

After its first year the Center grew from one room to two adjoining rooms. Emphasis shifted from independent sutdy to individual research, then to remediation, and then to a combination of all three. The Center is now able to offer a number of options to students, options which do not duplicate and do not compete excessively with classroom activities.

There was growing dissatisfaction during the first year because the opportunities of the Center were open to only selected students.

After vigorous discussions involving the staff and classroom teachers, it was decided to schedule all classes into the Center on a systematic basis, with each class and its teacher coming to the Center once a week. Some time was still reserved for groups with special interests or for those who needed individual work in depth. This move turned out to be very successful. Teachers began to gain a better understanding of the Center and ideas began to go back to the classroom. Materials and equipment were loaned to teachers for short periods of time. Teachers who now bring their classes to the Center and plan to use it effectively have a very successful experience. For at least one period a week (admittedly not enough, but all our resources allow), the teachers can choose to work with only one or a few students and let the Learning Center staff work with the others.

The Center attempts to promote independent study. It defines an independent learner as one who meets problems which he defines himself and for which he develops and carries out his own plan of attack. No grades are given in the Center and children are free to explore a wide variety of materials and games. We are encouraging a shift in the role of students from that of a spectator to that of an independent learner. We have encouraged teachers to shift from being directors of the learning situation to being mentors, critics, and finally colleagues in at least some situations for at least part of the school day. Emphasis has also been placed on replacing teacher-structured with student-structured curriculum materials, on moving from didactic to dialectic teaching methods, and on perceiving resources, including time and space, as variable, fluid and flexible.

Students work individually and in small groups on materials matched to their interests and needs. In one corner is a collection of attractively bound books written by the children in their own style. Typewriters at a small typing station with self-instructional books are in constant use. In another corner there may be a group of students studying together. There is an interchange of ideas and leadership moves from one child to another. Children take responsibility for orienting other children to the Center. There is much mutual help in learning, with students trying out new roles in a non-threatening environment. The child-to-child tutoring and helping program has been one of the consistently successful features of the Center. Sometimes these encounters are planned, with certain children selected to act as tutors or volunteer aides, but some of the best are unplanned, occurring when an older child spontaneously becomes involved with a younger one and works with him on a project. Often the older children, whose own classroom behavior sometimes leaves room for improvement, display patience, courtesy, and a strong sense of responsibility in working with the younger children.

Among the most popular offerings in the Center are the computer terminal and the keypunch machines. A consultant teaches classes in data processing and in computer languages (Fortran IV and Basic) for intermediate and upper grade students. We have been surprised and impressed by the number of ways in which students have used and responded to the computer equipment. It is relatively easy for an untrained student to call up one of a number of interesting word and logic games and to play it with the computer, usually with the "help" and advice of a few interested bystanders. We have found these games to be very effective in teaching language arts skills.

Another notable activity of the Center relates to the preparation of instructional materials. One of the mathematics consultants, for example, has been developing original, high-interest, largely non-verbal materials for use in the Center, particularly for children with high potential in mathematics but with reading difficulties that interfere with performance. This material has been made available to any Chicago school requesting it.

From time to time the Center has planned in-service programs for the Ray School teachers, showing them materials available in the Center and encouraging them to borrow materials for use in their classrooms. Three special days were planned for teachers to work with the mathematics consultant—a Fraction Day, a Decimal Day, and a Percentage Day. After an early morning demonstration for a large group of teachers, the consultant made appointments to see interested teachers while the Learning Center staff covered the teachers' classrooms. A series of informal workshops for teachers from six local public schools is projected, with the hope that ideas developed in the Center can be tried in regular classrooms in other schools in the area.

Special Projects and Events

Among the many special projects initiated by the Center staff was the teaching of Yoruba, a language of Western Nigeria, to a group of twenty-five interested black and white students. The teacher was a native Nigerian. In another project a Ray school parent teaches the poetry of a famous black poet. In a third project students write and bind their own books to be read by other students in the Center. Three large group assemblies have been sponsored in the school auditorium, one on Afro-American culture, a second on the story of young Dr. Martin Luther King, and the third, a slide presentation by a young muralist who had worked on many murals in Mexico and in the United States. Students from other schools were invited to these assemblies.

The Center organized a visit to the art history department of the University of Chicago for a group of students interested in the study of Greek civilization. The chairman of the department spent several hours with the group discussing aspects of Greek civilization and showing artifacts belonging to the university.

Another project grew out of the writing of a series of original African folktales by a consultant hired by the Center. Five students, three black and two white, were chosen to illustrate the book under the direction of a parent volunteer who is also a professional artist. After having read the first draft of the book, the student-artists went to museums to study artifacts from many African tribal cultures. They studied photographic reference material and then turned to the preparation of linoleum block prints to illustrate the book. We plan to print the book and distribute it at low cost to schools in the city interested in such work.

Help for
Individual Pupils

Many children have been helped in the Center because they were able to work on an individual basis with a skilled professional teacher who could give them the required time. One eighth grade student, for example, did well in all subjects but could not spell well. The Learning Center teacher worked closely with him over a period of time, helping him realize that he could improve his spelling, and that he could do it independently.

A bright seventh-grade black student had read many of the books and used much of the audio-visual material we have in our black studies section. He was very disturbed about how little black history was contained in his social studies texts. We enrolled him in a correspondence course in Afro-American history offered by a local museum.

Two recent arrivals to Ray school are Chinese children, a brother and a sister from Hong Kong. Both speak Chinese exclusively and both are hard of hearing. The supervisor of the special class where they were placed has worked closely with the Center staff. We were able to secure the services of a Chinese minister from a neighborhood church who agreed to work with the children three times weekly in the Learning Center.

A bright eighth-grade student, disenchanted with school, found an intense interest in the computer class. He worked at programming and other tasks, taught other students, and for the first time in years showed excitement in school.

A ten-year-old black student in the fifth grade was a chronic truant, fighting, sleeping, and uncooperative in class before coming to the Center. There he found a segment of school that he really liked and where he was somebody special. He and his ten brothers and sisters live in a small apartment. Home is often chaotic. One day, amidst all our activity and motion, he was asked what he liked about the Center. "It's a quiet place," he said.

An eighth-grade black student from Woodlawn was considered to be a low achiever who frequently disturbed others in the classroom. When he came to the Center the director was examining a recently arrived book containing many authentic old photographs of ordinary neighborhoods in Chicago, of historical landmarks, and of important institutions. The boy and the director looked at the book together, and thereafter he returned frequently to look at it further. He was astonished to find pictures of buildings in his own neighborhood. He was particularly impressed by a photograph taken from a balloon near the University of Chicago in 1907 and showing the Ray School. His enthusiasm for the book and its pictures spread to other eighth-grade boys.

Conclusion

Our experience shows that student behavior has changed since the Learning Center opened three years ago. Gang conflicts and tensions between black and white students have virtually disappeared. The Center can claim a share of the credit for these changes, along with the elimination of tracking and the leadership of the principal in efforts to reduce tensions among the students.

The inclusion of children from other schools in the Learning Center and in assemblies sponsored by the Center represents an endeavor that goes beyond our original plans. In our neighborhood there are four public schools, one of which is all black and another mostly white. Each of these schools had been an island unto itself. There are obvious human relations advantages to bringing children from the various schools together, and we are pleased with our progress in this area.

Because we are now working with nearly 800 children, all of whom visit the Center at least weekly, the task of reporting progress of the student to the teacher becomes at once more difficult and less necessary. For the students who continue to come on an individual basis, we have continued to give feedback to their teachers on their progress.

The main thrust of the Center has been to create activities which will have a continuing effect on the students, teachers, and environment of the school. By making learning enjoyable, by encouraging experimentation and exploration, by respecting children with all their varied talents and glaring faults, we have created a place where a child can find himself. The Center is designed to be an agent of change within and without the institution. It should be evaluated mainly on the basis of whether or not changes are in fact occurring. We believe they are. Within the context of a traditional elementary school we have demonstrated that children of different ages, abilities, races, and socio-economic backgrounds can achieve academically and contribute in a variety of ways to one another's development.

Perhaps the work of the Center is best reflected in the comment of a parent who visited us during a recent open house. After seeing the Center she said, "There's yet hope for urban education."

VII

Urban-Suburban Collaboration: The EdCo Experience

Robert W. Peebles and
Gordon A. Marker

In the greater Boston area, seven school districts have formed a collaborative which on the surface would appear to be an unlikely, if not an unhappy, union. The effort, now in its third year, runs the full gamut of social, economic, and educational problems facing large metropolitan areas. With Boston as the hub, the Education Collaborative (EdCo) includes such a range of diversities as 1) a three-fold difference in expenditures per pupil; 2) participation of parochial and private school people along with public educators, and 3) black and white enclaves of high unemployment and low income, along with other areas at the opposite end of the income spectrum.

The New England setting itself is a most formidable barrier in that it probably represents the greatest political fragmentation in the country. The Newton school district, for example, one of the six members of the collaborative outside Boston, is historically a collection of over a half-dozen separate communities. Boston itself has strong neighborhood or sectional feelings and rivalries which even urban renewal has been unable to destroy. For virtually every participating town there is close public scrutiny of school matters; the problems of local finance interlace school issues. Little fiscal autonomy exists and election to school committee membership may be the opening shot at political advancement.

The Education Collaborative for Greater Boston not only exists in a difficult environment, but it is thriving. It is apparently able to respond to educational needs in an extremely complex urban environment in ways which are relevant to the students as well as to administrators and parents. That it may meet some needs which are not unique to greater Boston and that it has developed a mechanism for providing educational services to a wide range of clients, may speak to its relevance for other areas. For our part, we feel that EdCo can easily be duplicated; thus, knowledge of what it is, where it is going, and by what approaches, may have general interest to the beleaguered educational community.

What Is EdCo?

Nearing completion of its third year, the Education Collaborative for Greater Boston is moving steadily from process to reality as a metropolitan model. The idea of urban-suburban collaboration in the Boston area was conceived in 1967-68 at the Harvard Graduate School of Education where seven superintendents agreed to submit a proposal for ESEA, Title III support. In September, 1968, EdCo was initiated under its present director with a mandate to plan and implement educational programs which link a large city, Boston, with six other communities which collectively represent a metropolitan slice.

The overall goal is to establish a metropolitan model in education that proves the viability of urban-suburban collaboration and the feasibility of an intermediate agency that works closely with the superintendent and staffs of member school systems. Programs deliberately designed to break down isolation, reduce educational inequities, mix urban and suburban children and staff, and involve the communities and the private sector have been planned and are now in operation. Such programs have demonstrated the pragmatic as well as the more obvious democratic and moral values of metropolitan and integrated education. The rationale for such collaboration, however, is not self-evident.

The EdCo Model

The EdCo approach to a metropolitan educational model is selective and rejects the argument that local autonomy must give way to a massive super-system. The EdCo model has evolved over a three-year period and is based on a few simple assumptions:
  1) Urban-suburban collaboration makes good *educational* sense quite apart from the social goals of teachers and administrators

to reduce insularity. We feel that a carefully developed program involving students from the various districts and/or providing services across district lines provides a better learning environment. Our preliminary investigations suggest that high quality and more diverse experiences can be supplied without materially altering costs.

2) Urban and suburban collaboration makes more likely the participation of "outsiders" in the educational process. The problems public education is supposed to redress do not originate with children, but with their parents. We insist, therefore, that it is necessary to blend diverse public and private resources to create the mix of energies necessary to effect educational solutions of lasting impact. EDCo, accordingly, sees itself as bringing together these resources to redress selected educational problems.

3) Fiscal benefits to the districts participating in the collaborative should be greater than through non-participation. We assumed areas for joint proposals could be identified which would provide funding not otherwise available. A modest investment by each district in EDCo, therefore, would yield substantially larger benefits in terms of services provided. Scale economies through collaboration would also be realized by selected pooling of services via EDCo.

Programs which have survived the rigors of EDCo's youth respond to needs and generally fit the assumptions discussed previously. Services directly to students and teachers in the EDCo systems have been the major emphasis during this period. Student services range from camp and annex school experience to involvement in a cooperative education program extending across district boundaries. Teacher services emphasize a small grants program and other encouragements to alternative forms of education such as workshops on the open classroom.

More recently EDCo is responding to needs in the administrative service and special services areas. Reading disability and special education, for example, are two new areas of service. EDCo will be designing and running a Reading and Learning Center for the EDCo schools and also conducting an experimental program to return selected special education students to general education classrooms. The scope of these services is described in greater detail in the following section.

Teacher Services

One of our concerns is with the many talented teachers who are acutely aware of the ills of our society and yet frustrated by their inability to have much influence in effecting educational reform. Much of this talent, moreover, is buried within large school systems or isolated in smaller school systems. Since there is no need for school boundaries to prevent the sharing of talent, EdCo operates a small grants program to encourage teachers to spread their innovations throughout the districts. We have awarded small grants to approximately seventy-five teachers totaling $30,000, an average of approximately $400 per teacher. These grants, directly affecting about 2,000 pupils, serve as a talent-discovering technique which brings together teachers from the seven school systems. These teachers have designed programs that increase city and suburban teachers' knowledge about each other, bring students from different areas into contact, develop new curriculum or approaches to learning, and generally foster urban / suburban collaboration. Some examples of the projects that teachers have designed include:

1) A six-month exchange program between Dorchester High in Boston and Concord-Carlisle High School in Concord, Massachusetts.

2) Elementary school students from a school in Boston participated in a science project with students from an elementary school in Newton which used the metropolitan area as a base for examining environmental conditions.

3) Another program saw high school students spend their vacation together with their counterparts from a suburban high school along with a mixture of teachers.

4) A teacher in Boston was able to use an EdCo grant to develop an elective advisory council of parents, students, teachers, and administrators for a junior high school which had been undergoing some severe problems. Although the school in question still has its difficulties, a remarkable improvement has occurred in the situation which existed there two years ago and the building principal credits much of the success to the new advisory group.

Closely related to the teacher innovative grants program is a series of workshops which focus on those techniques and issues which are directly related to current school needs as teachers attempt to reach students more sensitively and effectively. These workshops deal with such topics as the open classroom, the teacher and educational change, alternatives for urban education, promoting racial understanding, a metropolitan approach to environmental education, and the human relations approach to the drug problem. Each of these workshops involves a mixture of city and suburban teachers who benefit from the varying perspectives brought to workshops by teachers representing seven different systems.

Nearly 500 teachers from EDCO systems have gone through intensive workshops. The EDCO open classroom presentation also has been requested by non-member districts.

Student Services

Several EDCO programs have involved students from the city and the suburbs in a variety of experiences designed to kindle creative sparks rather than inhibit children. In an effort to make the classroom and school a much more pleasant place in which to be, EDCO developed a program in the performing arts. Children from four Boston elementary schools and their counterparts in two Cambridge schools and two Concord schools participated together in a sixteen-weeks program which brought young performing artists in music, ballet, opera, and theater to the classroom. The performers not only performed, but had children join them in workshops in the various arts. In keeping with the EDCO approach, the project mixed the urban and suburban children through bussing to a central location in Cambridge.

An evaluation of this project made possible by a grant from the U. S. Office of Education revealed that drama was effective in stimulating children to respond positively. The role-playing situations and the therapeutic value of acting out certain situations seemed to produce more understanding of the kinds of problems confronted within urban areas. Legitimizing emotions through the arts could be one of the most successful methods of motivating children to learn. By doing it within the framework of EDCO, children learn about and enjoy the arts in racially- and socially-mixed groups. The semester-long performing arts program was made possible by a $23,000 grant from a local charitable trust.

One of our most successful programs was the EDCO camp. Four sets of thirty boys, fifteen from the city of Boston and fifteen from a suburban school district, lived together for a week at a camp located twenty miles from Boston. The co-directors of this camp, one black, one white, with assistance from graduate interns, operated an exciting program for four weeks which included modified Outward Bound experiences, human relations training, science, and the usual outdoor camping activities.

The following anecdote was taken from a tape of one of the discussion sessions held in the barracks where these urban and suburban boys were reviewing their day's activities: "Whom do you trust among the people here?" "Him," one boy replied. "Why him? You didn't know him before today and he's a white kid and you're black." "Because he pulled me out of the swamp." By participating in experiences such as the "swamp walk" the boys began to understand each other as human beings. It is important to note that the students enjoyed the experience and felt that there should be more of this type of education in every school. The difference between the EDCO camp and the plethora of school camping programs is the imaginative metropolitan approach of the two directors who had gone away together for a week to plan the activities of the camp.

As a follow-up activity, EDCO has sponsored a metropolitan exchange program whereby many of the youngsters who had lived together at the camp were able to visit each other two days a week for a semester, sometimes in each other's schools, other times in each other's communities. Using the camera as a learning tool (the Polaroid Corporation donated thirty cameras), students were able to identify themselves more clearly and to relate themselves to others from within the metropolitan area. A deliberate attempt was made in this program (titled "Social Identity") to show the interrelatedness between a city and its outlying school districts.

For the first phase of an annex school program, EDCO will run a pilot storefront school in Boston. Students from two of the EDCO communities will join with Boston students, together with teachers from each of the participating systems, in the pilot program. The program, developed jointly by students and teachers, will be an important input in additional annex schools linking the city and the suburbs during the 1971-72 school year.

An annex school, as we see it, is a non-school space to which students will be sent for several weeks for the purposes of understanding a community other than their own and bringing students together from very different environments. The annex school thus becomes an alternative form of education, one which uses direct field experience as a way of learning academic subjects as well as the less traditional subjects. The students, for example, may study land use within a particular area, or may do a housing study and relate the findings to housing conditions in other neighborhoods. We see the annex schools as having counterparts in suburban communities so that there will be a two-way street which will allow students and teachers to provide curriculum guides or resources for use in EDCO system classrooms. The annex school idea is one which could expand rapidly and ultimately affect thousands of children.

Special Services

This past year EDCO added a special education component to its list of capabilities. It may prove to be one of the most important elements in our metropolitan model and has particular significance for cities where many children are assigned to special classes. The EDCO Special Education Project is developing new approaches in the field and is especially interested in moving educable children back into the mainstream of general education whenever and wherever possible. EDCO, consequently, has a program in four Boston schools for the training of teachers and paraprofessionals in a program to accomplish the above goals. There is much pragmatic value in a metropolitan approach to special education problems. It is impossible for most school systems to do an adequate job by themselves in such a complex area. By combining metropolitan resources, the chances of making breakthroughs in special education are much greater.

Another example of the work of the special education team is in the area of school-university relations. The universities in Greater Boston, including Boston University, Boston College, Northeastern, and Simmons College, are anxious to establish new models for their teacher trainees using EDCO as the vehicle to place these trainees in urban and suburban schools. This will allow future teachers to have both types of teaching experiences and should result in improved teaching / training programs.

Under EPDA funding, EDCO is operating a Black Recruitment and Training Program to provide additional staff for each of the seven EDCO school systems. The service will recruit blacks who are near certification but have not acquired it. It will also attract new teachers from other disciplines through provision of the marginal necessary support during the year of transition. In addition to a modest financial stipend, the EDCO program will provide on-going technical assistance to the teachers who may require such support. It is expected to bring about improved racial balance in teaching staffs as well as reduced staff development costs for the districts.

Summary

Some novel approaches can be developed where a few key conditions can be met. The superintendents have to feel a need to cooperate among themselves even if they cannot see exactly how it is to be done. The districts have to derive benefits in excess of costs, probably on the order of three-to-one. More important, the participating school districts should derive significant new monies, preferably from non-educational sources, which would not have been available without an EDCO. All of this, of course, spells improved services to students.

Above all, the superintendents and their boards have to trust in others who have a genuine interest in finding real solutions to problems common in whole or in part to all, whether in the city or the suburbs. Given this faith, even if it is partial and tentative, one can then begin the long and frustrating task of exploring the possibilities.

VIII

A Summer School for Understanding Metropolitan Living

Daniel U. Levine and Betty Hall

Look at our world today. What do you see? What are we faced with? Phrases such as "Where is Love?" "Is There Peace?" Problems and troubles all around us. We inherit an awful lot. We are the young. Passed down to us are the bad as well as the good and we must be prepared for it. We must know what to do, to keep history from repeating itself, again. This course will help us be prepared for the future.

Not many youngsters these days express the opinion that their courses in school are preparing them to meet the challenge of an uncertain urban future. But Mark Gomez, a ninth-grader in Kansas City, Missouri, was enthusiastically making just this assertion during the waning days of the summer before a new academic year started in September, 1970. He had just completed six weeks in the Summer School for Understanding Metropolitan Living (UML).

Understanding Metropolitan Living was a cooperative summer school sponsored and conducted by the Shawnee Mission School district in suburban Johnson County, Kansas, and the central city school districts in Kansas City, Kansas, and Kansas City, Missouri. A six-week instructional program was conducted between June 8 and July 17, 1970, for an intended enrollment of forty suburban students from Shawnee Mission and twenty students each from the two Kansas City districts.

Approximately half the students from each district were fifth- and sixth-graders enrolled in the elementary section and the other half were seventh-, eighth-, and ninth-graders enrolled in the junior high section. School district officials tried to select students who had demonstrated scholastic ability and had a record of good school attendance.

UML was a voluntary program which may have been the first of its type in the country to bring students together across state lines. It was made possible through a grant of $10,500 from Kansas City Association of Trusts and Foundations. Two elementary teachers and two junior high teachers were employed. Each team consisted of one white teacher and one black teacher.

During the first three weeks, when classes met in an elementary school in Shawnee Mission, the Kansas City participants were transported by bus to Shawnee Mission. During the second three weeks, Shawnee Mission students were transported to an elementary school in Kansas City, Missouri. Buses were available to take the elementary and junior high sections on the field trips which constituted a major part of the instructional program.

The Goals
of the Program

One of the important goals was to utilize community resources in learning about the metropolitan area and its people. The students were given a chance to learn about their own community in a context which encouraged them to recognize and understand both its strengths and its problems. The premises behind a program like UML are that it is desirable for a young person to take pride in his community, to feel a responsibility for working to improve it, to respect the accomplishments of people in other communities, and to develop a sense of obligation to work for the betterment of all the diverse groups in a highly interdependent metropolitan society. In addition to field trips and meetings with knowledgeable resource persons, students engaged in relatively unstructured discussions, viewed appropriate films, and used other types of learning materials. They thus gained much more first-hand understanding of the metropolitan area, its people, and their problems than normally can be acquired in a regular school program. In the elementary section, a large part of the curriculum was structured around the general theme "Urban Occupations." Teachers made a systematic attempt to help students become acquainted with the extremely diverse nature of the occupational possibilities open to them in a modern urban society. Discussions stressed the idea that all occupations require training and specific skills and that each job is important. The major field trips conducted as part of UML are shown in Table 2.

TABLE 2

List of Field Trips in UML

Elementary Program	Secondary Program
1. Inland Cold Storage	1. Overland Park City Hall
2. Court Trial	2. Overland Park Police Department
3. Douglass State Bank	3. Methodist Inner City Parish
4. General Motors Parts Division	4. Johnson County Courthouse
5. General Motors Factory	5. Kansas School for the Deaf
6. Fort Leavenworth	6. Shawnee Mission Board of Education
7. Children's Mercy Hospital	7. Shawnee Mission Northwest High
8. Shawnee Mission Park	School
9. University of Missouri at	8. Bonner Springs Agricultural
10. Kansas City	Hall of Fame
10. Fort Osage	9. Kansas School for the Blind
11. Manor Bakery	10. Johnson County Mental Health
12. Coca-Cola Factory	Association
13. Kansas City Star	11. Kansas City Model Cities Program
14. Swope Park	12. Cave Storage Industries
15. Kansas City Waterworks	13. Swope Park
16. Hub Afro-American Book Store	14. Jackson County Alcoholic Ward
17. Sears Roebuck	15. Kansas City Air and Water
18. Donnelly College	Pollution Control
Black History Display	16. Rehabilitation Center
19. Blue Valley Park	

A second important goal was to facilitate the development of positive intercultural understanding and intergroup relationships among students of different social, economic, racial, and ethnic backgrounds. Suburban students, ordinarily far removed from the tastes, sounds, and smells of the city, were provided with an opportunity to see the diversified character of a metropolitan area and to discover that it was not so remote after all. Central city students had an opportunity to learn about suburban communities and their inhabitants—an opportunity all too rare for central city children growing up in a large stratified metropolitan area. UML was seen as a way of reducing misunderstandings and barriers which arise when children of different groups are kept geographically and so-cially isolated. The program included recreational activities, a daily meal or snack, and various projects and social events—all designed to make UML a rewarding and satisfying group experience.

A third goal was to involve students actively in high-interest learning experiences dealing with the future of the metropolitan area. Particular emphasis was placed on helping students learn to take more responsibility for their own learning and on giving them opportunities to become more skilled in planning and carrying out learning activities. According to reports from teachers, the experiences planned by the junior high students included a bus trip through suburbia, a "yearbook" to be distributed to all participants, the making of a movie entitled "Friends," a UML newspaper, and an impromptu play which brought blacks and whites together in a common task.

Although it is not possible fully to describe on paper the aura of excitement in learning and the atmosphere of constructive cooperation in surmounting social and racial barriers, a feeling for the program can be obtained from the following excerpts from teachers' logs:

Monday, June 8, 1970. We attempted to alleviate the awkward period which we felt might exist during the getting acquainted session scheduled for the children and their parents. The first thing we did was to issue name tags to each parent and to each child. Secondly, each person was given a number, and each person was responsible for finding another who had the same number. Thirdly, coffee and sweets were provided, for we felt that some of our parents who had a longer distance to travel probably would not have had sufficient time to prepare breakfast. We also felt that eating might relieve some of the tension that might occur on such an occasion.

Monday, June 15, 1970. Most of the youngsters seemed more relaxed on the bus and more at ease with each other during our field trip than they had been the first week. Most of them chatted very freely and sang songs together.

Thursday, July 9, 1970. The Swope Park Bank was the first place we visited today. One student asked "Why would we visit a bank?" After the tour I asked one student if he felt that visiting the bank was a learning experience or a waste of time. He said, "They answered many questions that I had forgotten I was interested in, so I don't think it was time wasted." Another said, "I expected to see only black people working in the bank but instead we saw black and white people working together."

Monday, July 13, 1970. We have referred to air and water pollution during the numerous discussions. We decided to find out as many valid facts as time would permit. Our field trip to the Kansas City Water Works today was an outgrowth of our discussions on air and water pollution, which we had begun discussing on the bus one day.

. . . At the Water Works we had an extended tour and saw a movie on water purification. One student said, "Our tours get better all the time, this was one of the best." Another said "I would like to get more detailed information on air pollution." As a result we secured the film *What Are We Doing to Our World?*

Thursday, July 16, 1970. Today we went swimming at Shawnee Mission East. It was one of our best days . . . . No more than four or five of the black students could swim, but the white kids were trying to help them.

Monday, June 22, 1970. Today we worked in our various groups on the newspaper, on art and creative writing, and on courtesy. I observed more contact between black and white: sharing paints, helping one another on pictures or projects, asking for suggestions.

Evaluation of the UML

Student Reactions

In a program emphasizing student involvement in learning activities, it is important to determine whether students rate their experiences positively and whether they are motivated to engage in further learning. The responses of the elementary students to a questionnaire administered at the end of the UML program are shown in Table 3.

TABLE 3
Elementary Students' Responses to Selected Items on
"My Opinion of UML" Questionnaire

	Suburban Students			Central City Students		
	Yes	No	Blank	Yes	No	Blank
1. I liked going to Ray Marsh School	14	1	0	17	0	0
2. I liked going to Mary Harmon Weeks School	11	4	0	17	0	0
3. The bus ride was too tiresome	5	10	0	3	14	0
4. The teachers were friendly	14	1	0	16	0	1
5. It was hard meeting so many new kids	1	14	0	2	15	0
6. Most of the time I understood what the the teachers were explaining	14	1	0	17	0	0
7. I saw many things I had never seen before	14	1	0	16	1	0
8. I learn more in a regular classroom	4	11	0	8	9	0
9. I felt uncomfortable visiting different people in different parts of the city and suburbs	0	15	0	1	16	0
10. I found it interesting to study about other people	15	0	0	17	0	0
11. I learned new things about my own community	10	5	0	14	3	0
12. School would be better if all my classes were taught this way	11	4	0	13	4	0
13. Did you like having a "team" of teachers?	13	2	0	15	2	0
14. If UML is offered again in the future, would you like to join it?	15	0	0	17	0	0

An open-ended section of the questionnaire provided additional evidence of a positive and enthusiastic response to the program. Some of the comments were as follows:

Suburban junior high girl: "I never knew the city contained so many exciting things."

Central city junior high girl: "I liked going to places I had never seen before which was a great experience as well as education."

Central city junior high boy: "This course is indeed a full success. The people and teachers have made me learn in a different way and I like it."

Suburban elementary girl: "I thought colored people would be a little different from us but everybody is different I find out. It is fun."

Central city elementary boy: "I like meeting new boys and girls. I liked all the boys alike and different from our own race."

Suburban elementary boy: "I like the trips because I didn't know the things I saw and learned about. I thought the black people would be mean or something, but they weren't. They were very nice."

Student ratings of field trips, activities, and topics studied in UML were obtained. Students could check one of the following responses: "Liked very much", "Liked some," "Liked hardly at all," and "Did not like." For the elementary sample, fifty-seven percent of the 301 responses of central city participants and forty-eight percent of the 248 responses of suburban participants were in the "Liked very much" category, and there was only one activity on which the number of combined "Liked hardly at all" and "Did not like" responses equalled or exceeded the number of combined "Liked very much" and "Liked some" responses. For the secondary sample, response patterns were similar. For both samples the few instances in which a field trip or activity elicited almost as many negative as positive responses seemed to be experiences which provided little opportunity for active student involvement.

Parent Reactions

The perceptions of parents of UML students were obtained through an anonymous 19-item questionnaire. Responses to selected items are shown in Table 4. The responses show that parents held consistently positive perceptions. Responses indicating that their children were enthusiastic about the program and looked forward to attending were virtually unanimous. A substantial majority said their children had expressed a desire to enroll in UML if it were offered again.

TABLE 4

Parents' Responses to Selected Items on
"Evaluation of UML" Questionnaire

Item	Yes	No	Blank
1. My child was enthusiastic about the program	56	1	1
2. He or she discussed the activities freely	54	3	1
3. He or she looked forward to the program	57	1	0
4. He or she talked about new friends	53	4	1
5. He or she has indicated a preference to enroll in a summer school project again if another is offered	51	5	2
6. My child was invited to visit with a family outside the neighborhood	16	41	1
7. My child brought home a new friend from outside the neighborhood	6	51	1
8. My child seems more interested in the welfare of other people	48	7	3
9. My child seems more tolerant of other people's opinions	43	9	6
10. My child is more certain about his future	28	25	5
11. My child understands better now the way agencies provide services to the people of the community	51	5	2
12. My child shows greater respect for the ways different people make contributions to the larger community	51	2	5

Parents were also asked to indicate whether they would want their children to take part in UML if it were offered again. Of the 57 parents who responded, 51 said "yes," five said "no," and one said "possibly." Of the parents who did not respond affirmatively, two explained that their children would be too old or might not benefit as much a second time, one felt that a new group of youngsters should not be deprived of slots in the program, and one said that his child was less tolerant of other groups than he had been before UML. The remaining parents said they would enroll children only if participants could study more controversial and varied topics or could engage in service projects as part of the program.

It is possible that these data exaggerate the degree to which parents were positive about UML, inasmuch as parents with negative reactions might have been less likely to return the questionnaire. It is possible also, however, that parents were in a better position than staff members or researchers to obtain certain kinds of information about student reactions. We believe that responses to the parent questionnaire were generally very encouraging.

Teacher Reactions

Throughout the program teachers kept logs in which they described incidents and recorded their perceptions of the extent to which goals were being achieved. At the end of the program they filled out questionnaires to provide further information on this point. Teachers seemed to have little doubt that students were being helped to recognize problems existing in their own communities as well as in other communities in the metropolitan area. A teacher responding to the question, "Did the children grasp the idea of problems existing in communities other than the one they reside in?", wrote:

I believe they were quite concerned about this. We spent a lot of time discussing conditions in the Inner City Parish and the Model Cities Area. The suburban students thought the Model Cities idea of people helping themselves was good, and liked the idea of VISTA. Obviously, they could see their own problems as being minimal by comparison. They appeared to be very sympathetic to the needs of the underprivileged. Both blacks and whites were moved by what they saw.

Interracial
Relationships in UML

The students who participated in UML constituted a diverse group, including a Japanese-American girl, a Mexican-American boy, and others with a variety of ethnic backgrounds. Probably the most important characteristic of the student body was its balance between youngsters of Afro-American and European-American descent. The staff was especially interested in providing opportunities for black and majority white students to know one another and learn to cooperate in working out racial antagonisms deeply imbedded in our history and the current social scene. Except for this aspect of the program, every other objective of UML might well have been achieved in metropolitan-oriented summer schools conducted separately in the three participating school districts.

How well was this purpose achieved? The staff was particularly interested in knowing whether the students were working and cooperating with one another across racial lines. Verbal and written comments of the teachers indicated that interracial interaction and friendships were increasing as the summer progressed. But there were other indications as well.

Statements volunteered by students in interviews and written on the open-ended sections of the questionnaire provided some evidence of what was going on. The following are examples:

I found new friends and had a good friendship with them and found out that there are people who care.
I liked UML because it was a new and wonderful experience I will always remember and also because I learned that although it was two different races, we understood each other and had lots of fun together.
The experience of meeting new people is really something else. If

more people would come together we might not have the trouble the world has today. We have the burden on our shoulders. We've got to come together in order to change.

I never knew any black kids as friends. But now a lot of them are my best friends or just plain friends. The color of your skin doesn't matter. It is what's inside that counts.

Observations of the program and informal conversations with students made by the evaluation staff indicated that students frequently formed interracial sub-groups in academic as well as recreational activities.

A sociometric analysis of the elementary students' sixth-week responses to the question "Who are the three students in UML you would most like to be with in activities?" showed that thirteen of the fourteen white students present for testing chose at least one black student and eleven of the seventeen black students chose at least one white.

In assessing these data it is important to keep in mind that the purpose of UML was to provide experiences in which children would learn to work cooperatively and feel comfortable in interracial contacts. Individuals will sometimes prefer to interact mainly with others with similar social and ethnic backgrounds, and rightly so, since many people require intra-group experience to maintain a sense of individual security and self-worth. But no child or adult should have to avoid interracial contact simply because he has not had experiences to prepare him for such contact. The point is that each individual should feel free and should know how to enter into interracial situations—a goal which is not likely to be achieved unless young people of different races have opportunities to meet and become acquainted as individuals. UML was not wholly successful in this regard. There were some students who did not feel much more comfortable in interracial situations at the end of the program than they did at the beginning. There were some who kept almost entirely to their own racial group and participated only quite passively in interracial activities. It is possible that more planning time, and with teacher aides available, would enable the staff to increase the number of learning activities which would encourage active participation of each student.

Comments and Recommendations

Among the most important lessons we learned from our observations and data on UML for the summer of 1970 were the following:

1) Recruiting a good balance of black and white students may not in itself accomplish the goal of increased personal contact

among students of diverse socio-economic backgrounds. Since black students who volunteer to participate may tend to be drawn from relatively high status families, particularly those living on the outlying fringe of an inner city ghetto, special efforts must be made to recruit and enroll students from low status families in order to ensure wide representation from different social class groups.

2) Citizen and community initiative and cooperation from key central office educators are important factors in originating a program designed to increase pluralistic educational experiences for children in the metropolitan area. In the case of UML, much of the initial impetus came from members of local area school boards in Shawnee Mission and from members of the Church Without Walls in Shawnee Mission as well as the Education Committee of the Greater Kansas City Council on Religion and Race.

3) We believe a local college or university can and should play an important role in helping school officials initiate programs of this kind. Faculty and graduate students at the University of Missouri—Kansas City were involved in various stages of planning, implementation and evaluation. The university took the initiative in bringing outside consultants such as Dr. Lloyd Mendelson, Director of Project Wingspread, Chicago, to Kansas City to work with the four UML teachers. The university could also provide teacher aides for such a project as UML.

4) While this relatively small (eighty students) and short (six weeks) program was launched with relatively little advanced planning, larger and longer programs would almost certainly require substantial preparation and coordination. Even with the four outstanding teachers in UML it soon became obvious that they would have to stretch to the limits to make the program work in the absence of special training, advanced planning, and built-in time for on-going planning and evaluation.

5) Involvement of teacher aides and adult volunteers would provide the adult assistance needed to work with small groups in which withdrawn students would have more opportunity and encouragement to participate fully. In addition, aides and paraprofessionals could free the staff for daily planning sessions.

6) The UML teachers tended to feel that elementary students of both races were benefiting somewhat more from interracial contacts than were secondary students. This is apparently a common experience elsewhere. In terms of a cost-benefits analysis of a program like UML, it would probably be desirable to focus attention on elementary students if resources are limited.

7) Co-curricular actitivities (swimming, painting, ball games) were

viewed as an important part of the program by students from both the suburbs and the central cities. It would be a grievous mistake to view them as "frills" and cut them from summer programs designed to provide pluralistic educational experiences.

8) Successful community-based learning requires a careful weaving of field trips into a set of classroom experiences designed to teach definite skills, understandings, and attitudes. In most instances this can best be accomplished by developing appropriate themes, such as the Urban Occupations unit in UML, and by providing a suitable mixture of formal and informal learning activities related to the themes. UML probably did not offer enough formal lessons keyed to the field trips.

As evaluators whose task required us to become very familiar with UML, we will conclude with an observation we felt with increasing force as the program developed. At a time when individuals and groups are becoming so hostile and intolerant toward one another that the social order may be literally torn apart, we see little hope for the future unless Americans of all backgrounds work out a new Golden Rule to govern human relationships: "Although you are not exactly like me, I will not feel threatened but will accept and appreciate the integrity of your difference." If UML achieved anything at all for the students, it helped them recognize the value of their differences as well as the common humanity of their similarities.

IX

Outward Bound—
Education
Through Experience

Robert R. Lentz

OUTWARD BOUND is a month-long program for older adolescents. It is based on the belief that persons grow in the way they perceive both themselves and others—particularly others whom they might otherwise not choose to relate to in any human way—when they are put in a new environment and given a series of dramatic and challenging tasks which demand that they work together. Typically, participants in OUTWARD BOUND do work together and are successful to a degree they never thought possible. They find they feel good about each other in ways which take into account the peculiar set of individual characteristics which each one brings with him wherever he goes.

Through a carefully programmed use of an essentially natural environment OUTWARD BOUND allows a participant an opportunity to come to a series of important awarenesses about himself, his relationships with others, and his inter-relatedness with natural forces. The program emerges out of a definite set of assumptions, which include the following beliefs:

1) value of personal confidence based on individual success
2) reality of human inter-dependency
3) human inter-action which grows out of group responsibility and group accomplishment is essentially honest, useful, and healthy
4) value of an intensive confrontation with fundamental natural forces
5) value of extended solitude and contemplation

6) value of performing meaningful service
7) much can be learned when problems are presented rather than answers given
8) maturity entails, among other things, having had real experience with a wide range of natural human emotions—fear, joy, fatigue, respect, hunger, laughter, pain, love.

OUTWARD BOUND developed out of rather dramatic circumstances on the Atlantic Ocean in the early days of World War II. British ships were regularly being torpedoed, and British sailors were regularly abandoning ship, searching out available life boats, and awaiting the uncertain arrival of rescue vessels. In these circumstances, it was found that the life expectancy of the younger, apparently more physically-fit seamen was significantly less than the life expectancy of the older, apparently less fit seamen. One reason which was advanced to explain this phenomenon was that the older men tended to last longer in difficult situations because over the years they had acquired enough experience to recognize that they had staying capacities and inner strengths upon which they could rely in times of serious stress. The younger men, it was reasoned, simply hadn't had enough experience to convince themselves of their own capacity to endure. The young men, therefore, simply gave in and submitted, even in some cases jumping out of life boats.

Out of this concern for sailors' lives, an educator and an owner of a steamship company developed an intensive program particularly aimed at giving the participants the psychological equivalent of those "life experiences" which the younger seamen lacked and which were so critical to their very survival. The program's participants were given an increasingly complex series of demanding physical tasks. It was hoped that through a continuous process of succeeding in confronting the difficult, these participants would learn they could indeed overcome both physical and psychological fear. It did turn out that the life expectancy of the merchantmen trained in this way was significantly increased. This was the beginning of the OUTWARD BOUND program.

Since World War II, the program has concerned itself with enhancing the ability of its participants fully to survive not only physically, but also emotionally and socially. OUTWARD BOUND came to the United States in 1962. It has flourished here as it has taken on a peculiarly American flavor, while at the same time keeping rather close ties with the goals of its originators.

The Program

OUTWARD BOUND schools are located in Colorado, North Carolina, Maine, Minnesota, Oregon, California, and New Hampshire.

Another program will be started soon in Texas. While each program differs somewhat because of the particular environment which is used, there are a series of programmatic elements which are regularly a part of an OUTWARD BOUND experience wherever it occurs. Some of these elements include:

1) *The Wild Walk* Shortly after arrival, the entire group of seventy to 100 persons is broken into units of ten or so and take off for a rather singular tour of the area immediately adjacent to the school. The tour takes several hours. It usually involves running, walking, and immersion in the natural environment. In Minnesota, for instance, the participants will be led through the woods, across a swamp (usually complete with a magnificent mud-fight), through a marsh, a thicket, and across a rapidly-flowing stream. In this process, the participants from time to time need to hold hands, and give support to each other. They must stay in touch with the people in front and behind and share responsibility for each other. At the end of the walk, they emerge muddy, dirty, wet, tired and predictably ecstatic; after all, they have gotten through, and in the process they've made very sure that the instructors were also muddy, dirty and tired.

   The effect of the event at the beginning of a course is often a profound one in that it clearly informs a participant that he is in a new world where old habits of action and thinking don't necessarily have the same currency as they did in the old one. This initial experience begins to establish the conditions necessary for significant reassessment and growth. From the beginning, the OUTWARD BOUND experience is designed to be a real one, a possible one, and an interdependent one.

2) *Initiative Tests* Initiative tests are problems given to individual groups of ten participants. The most easily described problem consists of a bare fourteen-foot wall which the participants are asked to get everyone over. This is a problem which allows the group, with the assistance of an instructor, to focus on a number of questions that it must deal with in other ways on longer, more difficult, and less clearly defined tasks.

   The group will be given the problem and several enthusiastic leader-types will rush forward and begin to push people up and over the wall. Some other person, meanwhile, will be looking at the problem and thinking maybe there is a better way, perhaps even saying rather quietly that he thinks there might be another way. The energetic leader-types finally are confronted with the realization that they are not going to get the last person or persons over, and so they dash into other alternatives. At this time someone perhaps hears that the quiet thinker has an idea; he then gets the others to stay still and listen to the new idea and tries to see that the group operates on the basis of the new in-put.

Once the group is over the wall, accomplished by a great deal of pulling, handling, jumping, and catching, there is an opportunity to discuss the wall-problem and the way the group dealt with it. Leadership can be discussed, as can decision making. The group can discuss the obligations of some to speak out more, and others to listen more. In many cases the wall serves as a means through which the group begins to come to an increased awareness and acceptance of different physical, and intellectual capacities.

3) *Expeditions* A good bit of time is spent during each OUTWARD BOUND course acquiring both the set of skills and a style of operating which will allow the group successfully to complete its final expedition—a four- to six-day journey from one point to another accomplished without an instructor. The necessary skills and capacities include knowledge of first aid, increased physical fitness, competence with map and compass, and the ability to cook, handle rope, and predict weather. Each group must also learn how to organize itself so that it can get up and get started quickly and make decisions along the way. None of these skills is taught in the abstract; instead, they grow naturally out of situations which arise during various preliminary expeditions and training exercises during which the instructor is present—though less conspicuously as the course progresses.

4) *Rock Climbing* Each school's program includes several sessions of technical rock climbing on escarpments which are located in the vicinity of the school. Rock climbing generates a highly dramatic confrontation with one's own fears as well as a tremendous exhilaration upon completion. Interdependency is an essential characteristic since each climber is always "delayed" by a fellow participant upon whom the climber is dependent should he slip and begin to fall. Each student is given a variety of routes to climb so that he can achieve both success and failure, at least to the degree that these are measured by getting to the top.

5) *Solo* Each OUTWARD BOUND course includes three days spent alone in the wilderness with no food, a journal, and only basic clothing and shelter. This solo experience usually comes near the end of the program. Solo is often a rather powerful personal

experience coming as it does just after an intense group experience. Solo can be viewed in a number of ways. A participant can choose to view Solo primarily as a survival exercise, an opportunity to work hard at living off the land. He can also view it primarily as an opportunity for personal assessment or as a time to catch up on sleep, to experience a bit of hunger, or to be generally glad that the active part of OUTWARD BOUND is off his back. Some participants find the three days to be the most boring experience of their lives, while others find it the most fearful thing they've ever done. Whichever the case, each student has a chance to find out what he can make of three days in the wilderness with himself, nature, some paper, and a pencil.

6) *Evaluation* There is no formal evaluation of a participant's OUTWARD BOUND experience, at least not in the sense of having the experience reduced to a discrete set of criteria which are measured either subjectively or objectively. A good bit of use, however, is made of several kinds of feedback.

Each participant obviously gets some feedback that may or may not be significant every time he is involved in an activity, be it the Wild Walk, Rock Climbing, or Solo. In addition to feedback from these events, he gets what is often very significant feedback to his behaviors and attitudes from various members of the group. The participant also keeps a journal which often serves as a means through which he objectifies his experience and sorts out the mass of stimuli that affect him daily.

These informal approaches are supplemented by several more formal approaches. Each instructor spends some time with each participant at regular intervals during the course. The participant is asked to discuss and to evaluate his experience in terms of his goals and expectations. The instructor may suggest some questions which the participant might want to consider. At the end of the course, the instructor confers with each participant. This conference includes a discussion of the total program's impact upon the participant.

Each group of students also confers either with the school's director or the course director. Here the group as a whole comments on the total collective experience and considers its strong and weak points, including those which relate both to the staff and to the program.

Each participant receives a report, usually in the form of a personal letter from his instructor, which restates in a positive manner some of the key points they've discussed during the course. The report is seen as an up-beat statement which serves to transfer the

OUTWARD BOUND experience from the wilderness environment to the student's more civilized home environment.

The Make-up
of the Group—
Some Apparent Lessons

As participants within an OUTWARD BOUND program grow and develop, so has the total OUTWARD BOUND program grown during the last ten years. It consistently undergoes re-examination to see if there are better ways to reach the stated goals. OUTWARD BOUND clearly has made some significant changes in the structuring of its program in the expectation that the program will consistently be a more successful multi-racial, multi-cultural experience.

From the beginning OUTWARD BOUND in the United States has operated under an internally imposed guideline which says that fifty percent of the participants of each course should be scholarship students. This guideline grew out of the belief that the kinds of growth that OUTWARD BOUND hopes to achieve at both the personal and the inter-personal level can best take place within a group which is as diverse as is reasonably possible. Stated in a different way, OUTWARD BOUND operates on the assumption that people learn and grow when they confront and come to terms with not only a different physical environment, but also with a varied social environment.

The scholarship guideline was imposed in large part because it was felt that a heterogeneous group would serve to break down a number of stereotypes which operate in our culture. This commitment to heterogeneity led to some amusing and some frustrating situations. Some schools carefully sorted application blanks according to as many criteria as they could identify. Students thus were divided by age, weight, race, type of school, type of community, whether the mother or father signed the application blank, whether tuition-paying or scholarship, and in some cases whether or not applicants were referred by juvenile authorities. According to OUTWARD BOUND's thinking at that time, the ideal patrol would therefore include one black, one Indian, one prep-school white, one migrant worker, one detention home referral, one fat, one thin, and an even distribution of scholarship versus tuition-paying students as well as mother-signed versus father-signed applications.

We discovered, of course, that applicants did not always fall into such neat categories. The whole process was thrown off by applications which came from prep-school detention-home referrals, or from tuition-paying urban Indians. Not only did the applicants refuse to fall into our neatly-defined categories, but the desired heterogeneity was almost never reached. What regularly happened was that a group of ten participants would consist of five white upper-middle-class participants, several middle-class whites on partial scholarships, one urban black on full scholarship from Title I funds, and somebody else thrown in for good measure. At the time, OUTWARD BOUND administrators felt good because the scholarship students were there and a cross-section of American life was present. Therefore, so the reasoning went, growth would occur and stereotypes would dissolve.

It was soon discovered, however, that a few unanticipated things were happening. First off, OUTWARD BOUND found that for the urban disadvantaged participant, the entire OUTWARD BOUND experience was much different than it was for the middle-class participant. The middle-class participant often had regularly been exposed to the outdoors in at least some minimal way, and even if he hadn't, he tended to have a wider range of experiences which allowed him to feel more comfortable in a strange situation than did a low-status student. The social milieu in the OUTWARD BOUND group was one which usually was decidedly middle-class, with all the accepted values and customs we have come to associate with that term. Many minority group participants therefore were involved in a program that was much more anxiety-producing for them than it was for many of the other participants.

The drop-out rate for minority group members was quite a bit higher than it was for other students. This higher drop-out rate tended to accomplish exactly the opposite of what OUTWARD BOUND had hoped would be accomplished. Stereotypes became reinforced within the group, and individual self-images often were negatively reinforced. Not surprisingly, some questions were raised about OUTWARD BOUND's assumptions and procedures. The staff began to recognize that it was asking members of a minority group to operate within a culture and a value system that was pretty much set by a middle-class consensus usually arrived at unspokenly.

Some changes have been made. The first and most important is that in every situation where it is possible, the staff sees that those groups which have racial minority participants have at least forty percent racial-minority participation. Some groups in the same course thus will have no minority group participants, and other groups will have approximately forty to fifty percent minority participation. Under this arrangement each participant is more likely to find within his group some members who identify with his own subculture; thus, he is more likely to find a sense of support in times of personal stress and anxiety. The awareness that support is present often gives the participants the confidence to reach out across racial and cultural barriers and relate with all members of the group as individuals. This change in group composition has led to a much higher percentage of minority participants completing the course. Beyond the change in group composition, OUTWARD BOUND has also provided some fairly extensive training for its staff so that it can be more aware of and sensitive to the different impacts which the same event can have on participants from different backgrounds.

Programs Run in Affiliation with Outward Bound— Some Examples

Some school districts have regularly sent groups of students and faculty to OUTWARD BOUND. Other institutions have taken from OUTWARD BOUND a series of concepts and programmatic ideas and applied these to their on-going program in ways that have produced both solid academic gains and positive interracial experiences.

In some cases in which OUTWARD BOUND has worked with school systems, OUTWARD BOUND and the school system have shared funding sources, staff, and responsibility for programmatic design. In other cases, OUTWARD BOUND, the school system and an affiliated college or university have shared the responsibility for exploring the educational ramifications of the developing program. Two of these programs are described on the following pages.

East High School, Denver, Colorado (Robert Colwell, Principal)

This school has been going through a process with which many urban high schools are well acquainted. It draws students from an attendance area that until the mid-sixties was almost entirely white middle-class and college-oriented. New high schools were built though, the population began to move, and schools were re-districted. East High, as a result, is now approximately forty percent black, fifty percent white, and ten percent Hispano and Oriental.

East High has worked long and hard to become an educational institution which recognizes, values, and respects the individual and cultural differences which enrich learning. The school today is a remarkable example of what can be done when efforts are made to provide a meaningful education within a climate which recognizes the need for and the values implicit in cultural diversity—a diversity in which there are many commonalities, but in which each person is free to express himself and his heritage in ways which give his life richness and meaning.

OUTWARD BOUND and East High have collaborated in many specific ways, culminating in the creation and the implementation of the Senior Seminar. This seminar includes several innovations: 1) full-time field study for an entire term; 2) multi-disciplinary team teaching; 3) intensive group living; 4) implementation of OUTWARD BOUND activities at the term's beginning as a process through which to develop group cohesion and understanding, and 5) a culminating experience in which the whole program is both supplemented and synthesized.

At the beginning of the involvement neither OUTWARD BOUND nor East High School could foresee the educational ramifications of their relationship. During the three years previous to the seminar, between thirty and thirty-five of East High's faculty had been directly involved in at least one OUTWARD BOUND activity. These activities ranged from thirty-day, accredited summer teacher practice to rafting trips and human relations seminars (three days in the wilderness and three days in the city spent talking, visiting, being talked to). In addition to faculty involvement, more than three hundred students had been involved in a similar set of activities.

The Senior Seminar in many ways grew out of the sense of confidence and competence which resulted from the faculty's increased involvement in out-of-school educational techniques. The seminar was staffed by a combination of contract teachers from East High, student teachers from a nearby university, a Vista volunteer, and a staff of college student-tutors. The Seminar participants were 100 students in the last term of their senior year, chosen to reflect the racial heterogeneity of the school. A target group of low achieving or poorly motivated students identified by their counselors as having college potential were also included. The college tutors worked especially with this target group. The tutors not only assisted the students academically, but also encouraged the students to explore opportunities for post-high school education and helped the students to obtain and fill out application and scholarship forms. (The previous year, scholarship funds which were available to East High students had gone unused because of a lack of applicants).

The Senior Seminar students spent the term in a variety of two-and-a-half-week modules which included an OUTWARD BOUND module as well as modules in urban arts, politics and power, Hispano culture, space technology and man, and Navajo culture. The final module consisted of a rafting trip on the Green River which included a serious exploration of the geology, the history, and the anthropology of the area. Academic credit was given for earth science, history, art, literature, and, in several cases, consumer mathematics.

A rather extensive set of evaluative measures were used to assess the program. These measures ranged from questionnaires to participants and their families to pre- and post-student attitude surveys and forced choice opinionnaires. All measures indicate that the students judged the seminar successful, and that their attitudes had moved in directions consistent with the design of the program.

The participating students had a much lower drop-out rate than their peers, and almost all the target students enrolled in some form of post-secondary education, with the great majority of them going to either a university or to a junior college.

The letter of transmittal which went along with the seminar report to the Denver Board of Education contained some impressive words from the school's principal. "We are proud of the seminar because it met and exceeded most of our objectives. The verbal and statistical report we recommend to your study. . . . It does not and cannot interpret, however, the personal growth, the cultural transformation, the cross cultural enrichment, the new communications skills, the patience with and working knowledge of our political and social structures which the students learned."

The Senior Seminar is an on-going program, one which once again will deal with only a hundred students out of over 2,000. However, both the faculty directly involved with the program and the administration of the school are working hard at exploring the implications of the seminar for the total educational program at East High.

Trenton High School
Action Bound Program
(Phillip Costello, Director)

Trenton High School is the single high school for the city of Trenton. It sits exactly on the border between the city's black area and its ethnic area. Not unexpectedly, the school has had to deal with the tensions that have emerged between these groups over the last several years. It is heavily policed and very much security-conscious. In this setting, the Action Bound program was introduced.

This program has focused primarily on those students who were dropping out of school either physically, psychologically, or emotionally. During the past year, however, the program has come to deal with more than this one group, to the benefit of all.

The Action Bound program is multi-dimensional and is based in large part on the belief that students have to be involved in real things that have both immediate and long-range importance. The staff clearly recognized that the participant's self-image had to be increased, and that the students had to come to know that they could play positive roles in the world.

The nucleus of the staff consisted of several regular OUTWARD BOUND instructors as well as OUTWARD BOUND-trained instructors. The program's many elements have attempted to relate the wilderness skills and experiences to the everyday world of the city of Trenton.

Some of the programmatic elements that emerged were:

1) The creation of a rescue unit which was well trained in wilderness rescue techniques and first aid. The unit had to be prepared to be called out at any time and has been, in fact, called out from school several times.

2) The development of a biology-physiology course around the first aid skills which are a part of the rescue work. This course also involved some specific training given by the fire department and the police department.

3) The use of many of the participants by a local hospital as paid orderlies in the emergency room. There the boys helped greet patients, calm them, transport them, and take them to the morgue when the doctors could be of no further use.

The participants also regularly took part in week-end excursions to go rock climbing, spelunking, and canoeing.

After several years of week-end programs, many of these outdoor elements were moved into the regular week's curriculum as an optional program called "A Day In Another Environment." This program is open to students from any part of the school. Here impressive understandings have come about as students from the various tracks were given an opportunity to interact in some new ways—ways which involved both an academic component and a human relations component.

Another aspect of the Action Bound Program involves arranging for the participants from the black neighborhood and the ones from the white neighborhood to spend alternate week-ends giving the others a tour of their own neighborhood, explaining what is going on, who the various leaders are, and what the area's problems are. This design has been carried over to a program of teacher training at a local college in which the participants from Trenton High School spend time with the teachers in the outdoors of New Jersey before they work together in the inner city. This program has given the boys a new understanding of their own neighborhood as well as a feeling of self-worth and importance because for once *they* are the experts.

An evaluation of the Action Bound Program completed several years ago by a team of researchers from Princeton University concluded in part that "the inner-city disadvantaged students began to develop as a consequence of their OUTWARD BOUND training those attributes of character which act as a foundation for achievement motivation and for mature social participation."(1)

Conclusion

OUTWARD BOUND is an educational process which regularly brings people together so that they may grow in terms of their understandings of themselves, of others, and of society. These goals are ones often talked about at commencement time, bond issue time, and in civics classes. The rhetoric, however, has often served to cover over the lack of vital programs which actually function in an effective way to develop students who are secure in themselves, who are able to relate well and honestly with their neighbors, and who have the ability to function in society in ways that are both productive and personally fulfilling.

The programs which OUTWARD BOUND runs at its schools across the country for boys and girls 16½ and over and for interested adults can help in the creation of a citizenry which is mature, compassionate, and active. No program, however, which is several weeks long can legitimately claim to be able to achieve these important ends in and of itself.

Such a program may, however, demonstrate some basic principles which can serve as foundation stones for the development of a more effective curriculum. OUTWARD BOUND is seriously interested in exploring the implications and the ramifications of its approach for education across the country as the nation's schools attempt to come to grips with human and social questions that are peculiar to this part of the twentieth century in this part of the world, as well as with those questions which seem to be forever with us as man attempts to deal with his basic wishes, needs, and dreams.

Note

(1) Harold M. Schroeder and Robert E. Lee, *Effects of Outward Bound Training on Urban Youth*, Princeton University, n.d.

X

Individualization
and Non-Grading
in an Integrated
Elementary School

Leonard S. Kidd

Fremont Elementary School is one of some 120 elementary schools in the San Diego Unified School District. San Diego Unified has a K-12 enrollment of 129,572 students. Of this total enrollment, 12.5 percent are members of the black ethnic minority while 10.6 percent are of Mexican-American origin. The large balance of students are classified "Other White."

Fremont Elementary is situated in the Old Town district of San Diego, California, where there remain vestiges of the early Spanish influence. It was here, in the Old Town area, that San Diego and California had their beginnings in 1769. Fremont is a small elementary school with a total K-6 enrollment of 270 students. Of this number twenty percent are black, twenty-three percent are brown (based on Spanish surname) and the balance white. This ethnic balance is achieved by transporting fifty-five black children from Southeast San Diego and approximately fifty-five white children from North San Diego. Approximately 160 children live in the immediate vicinity of the school.

Busing has been undertaken only on a voluntary basis. Both black and white children are bused from two different communities into a third neutral area approximately half-way between the black and white geographic areas. Busing of pupils for the past three-year period has been successful at Fremont School due to several reasons. The instructional program at Fremont has been sufficiently enriched to warrant having children travel up to sixteen miles round trip each day. Competent adult monitors ride the buses and maintain a good social atmosphere. It is important to note that pupil turnover among the bused pupils is considerably lower than it is for the rest of the school's pupil population.

Model School Program

During summer 1968, the Board of Education approved a proposed plan for a model school program to be conducted at Fremont School. The program was designed to test on a pilot basis: 1) nongrading as an organizational plan; 2) abandonment of traditional grouping patterns; 3) an attempt to individualize learning, and 4) integration achieved by busing.

Selection of students for participation in the model school program was done on a voluntary basis. Parents were notified by letter of the intent to conduct the program and those interested submitted applications. A placement committee selected the participants. For the first two years of the program applicants were chosen primarily on a first-come, first-served basis. Selection for the third year was done more selectively. District counselors interviewed teachers and principals of the sending schools of each child whose parents had submitted applications. Selective screening appeared to be necessary since a large number of children who had severe learning or behavior problems were being admitted from other schools. The model school provided a natural attraction for parents and children who were discontented with their neighborhood school. An attempt is continuing to recruit a balanced enrollment.

The total involvement of the Fremont staff has been very important to the success of the model school program. This involvement began with a two-week workshop for which the faculty was paid on an hourly basis at the same rate of pay as curriculum writers. Attendance by faculty members was encouraged but was placed on an optional basis permitting those who had previous commitments to keep them. As it turned out, almost total staff participation was achieved.

Throughout the course of the three-year period during which the program has been in effect, the principal and other administrative officers of the district have made every attempt to include the total staff in decision making. It has been the purpose of the principal to develop a spirit of teamwork and consensus decision making in the staff. This has resulted in a commitment on the part of the staff to the program and a feeling of responsibility for its success.

At the outset of the program, teachers were given a choice of remaining at Fremont or of transferring to another school within the district. All of the teachers chose to remain in the program. The regional director and principal cooperatively selected three additional teachers and extended them invitations to participate in the program. Attention was given to the idea of selecting an ethnically balanced staff corresponding to the ethnic mixture of the student enrollment. This was achieved in the selection of the three new teachers.

Summer Workshop Program

The 1968 summer workshop began without a fully planned agenda, thus allowing the agenda to evolve from the participants. High priority was given by the faculty to the following items:
1) The meaning of nongradedness and the development of a rationale for this plan of organization.
2) How to achieve compatible grouping structures within a nongraded plan of organization.
3) What is the meaning of individualized learning and how is it achieved?
4) What instructional materials are needed for the individualization of learning?
5) How can instructional aides be most effectively used in the instructional program?
6) How can teaming or the redeployment of pupils best be used in a nongraded school?
7) How can parents best be informed of the objectives and nature of the program?

Discussion during the first days of the workshop centered mainly on the concept of nongradedness. Several members of the group had been exposed to the ideas of Goodlad and Anderson and one or two people were acquainted with the work of Madeline Hunter, principal of the U.C.L.A. laboratory school. Out of these discussions evolved a rationale for nongrading which included the following concepts:
1) Allows for mobility of pupils and flexibility of instruction.
2) Helps to develop the learner as an individual and as a member of a democratic society.
3) Removes the rigid grade lines, allowing the curriculum to be organized into vertical levels of learning through which a child can progress at his own rate.

4) Minimizes failure because each child works at his own rate.

The faculty settled on a three-age-level grouping for each classroom. Primary rooms were organized with approximately equal numbers of six,- seven,- and eight-year-olds while the upper grade classes were made up of nine,- ten,- and eleven-year-olds. A bridging room was provided which was composed of eight,- nine,- and ten-year-old children.

Homogeneous versus heterogeneous grouping within each classroom was discussed. Without exception, the faculty agreed that the children should be heterogeneously grouped but that some attention be given to the range of achievement between the highest and lowest achievers. It was difficult for most of the members of the faculty to abandon traditional grouping structures, but it also was necessary to avoid grouping practices which might result in racial segregation within the classroom. Finally, the grouping structure illustrated in Figure 1 was adopted.

FIGURE 1: GROUPING STRUCTURE

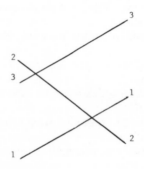

The slanted line numbered 1 represents six-year-olds or first graders, while the lines labelled 2 and 3 represent second and third graders. The lines are slanted to show the gradation of achievement levels in reading with the lowest achievers falling toward the lower end of each line by grade and the highest achievers being placed nearer the higher end of the line. The composition of the classes can now be envisioned, based on reading ability measured by a standard reading test. Classroom A was composed of a group of first graders whose reading scores fell within the lowest one-fourth of all first grade reading scores. Second graders assigned to classroom A were among the highest one-fourth of second graders in reading achievement. The third graders assigned to classroom A were low-achievers. Classroom D was similarly composed of first graders whose reading scores were within the top one-fourth of all first grade reading scores. Second graders were among the lowest one-fourth of second graders in reading achievement. The third graders assigned to classroom D were high achievers. From the diagram the reader can infer the achievement levels of the two groups in classrooms B and C.

The faculty believes that this plan of assigning children to classes accomplished three important things. First, it provides heterogeneity based on achievement in reading. Second, it allows compatible grouping within the class when needed. Third, it minimizes segregation arising from the fact that minority students generally have been more educationally disadvantaged than majority students.

Individualized Learning

Individualized learning has been discussed frequently since our program began and each teacher has made a valiant effort to accomplish a high degree of individualization in the classroom. In the beginning we had a tendency to think of individualization as "doing something different for each child." We eventually revised our definition to include "not necessarily doing something different for each child, but doing something appropriate for each child."

To accomplish the goal of individualized learning, it seemed appropriate that we consider employing paraprofessional aides to assist in the instructional program. For the first year of operation two paraprofessionals per classroom were employed. One of these people was a teacher assistant, who by district designation is a college junior or senior. The other aide was a parent or other adult hired out of the district in which the pupils live.

The goal of each teacher, with regard to the use of instructional aides, has been that of keeping the services of the aides as close to the pupils as possible. The responsibilities of the aides have ranged from small group instruction of pupils to tutoring individual pupils, following the guideline that, "It is the teacher's responsibility to initiate instruction and the aide's responsibility to carry out the teacher's plans." Clerical-type tasks have generally been de-emphasized.

After the first year, the use of aides was evaluated and it was apparent that teachers were having difficulty managing the schedules of two people in addition to their own. It was then decided that the position of teacher assistant would be dropped. Since that time, assignment of an instructional aide in each classroom has worked very well. Teachers feel that this facet of the program contributes greatly to our goal of individualization. It also increases opportunities to place interracial teams in classrooms where pupils can watch adults of differing racial background work together on common tasks.

The in-service training opportunities provided by the school and school district have proved important in ensuring success in the use of instructional aides. This in-service training has focussed on student discipline and control, use of audio-visual equipment, child growth and development, management of small group instruction, and intergroup relations. Three of the instructional aides are enrolled in a Career Opportunities Program pursuing teaching credentials. Others have taken courses offered by the junior college for instructional aides.

Programmed instructional materials and materials that lend themselves to individualized learning methods have proved very useful. Sullivan Programmed Reading Materials are used at both primary and upper grades. These materials enable teachers to place each pupil in the program at his own level of achievement and allow each child to progress at his own rate. Each classroom also has a Science Research Associates Reading Kit which handily supplements the Sullivan basal program. Harper and Row reading materials are also available to the teachers and are used with those pupils who complete the highest level in the Sullivan series.

The state-adopted Houghton-Mifflin mathematics series is heavily supplemented with individualized materials. Representative of these materials is the Singer Drill and Practice Kit. These kits are available for use in grades three through six. Sullivan Programmed Mathematics materials are also used with lower achieving pupils, primarily as remedial materials. The focus of the materials is on computation. Drill tapes are used to facilitate the learning of arithmetic basic facts. The tapes are kept in the learning resource center and their use is supervised by an instructional aide who is assigned there.

Learning Resource Center

The learning resource center is of tremendous value to our individualized learning program. The space occupied by the learning center is a regulation classroom. Individual study carrels encourage pupils to study and do individual research. A built-in cubicle in one corner provides a space for isolated group work. Several centers of interest are appropriately placed in various parts of the room. A wealth of resource materials, such as transparencies, study prints, and filmstrips are available. Typewriters, bioscope, and listening centers are available for pupil use.

The instructional aide who staffs the center five hours each school day is vital to the success of the learning center. The aide supervises the use of materials and equipment, works with small groups of children on special projects, obtains additional materials for teachers from the district's instructional aids center and is generally responsible for the proper use of materials and equipment. Scheduling of pupils for use of the center is done in an unstructured way. A sign-up schedule is provided but usually arrangements for use of an area within the center are made orally by the classroom teacher and learning center aide.

Fremont teachers have given considerable attention to the development of an appropriate climate for learning in each classroom. Our goal is to reach that fine point of balance between permissiveness and structure. The teachers are attempting to help their pupils develop greater self control and more self direction in their learning tasks. Children feel free to move about the classrooms for purposeful activities. Trips to the school library and learning resource center provide relief from the more highly organized classroom activities.

The teachers have organized the curriculum in large blocks of time. The daily schedule is flexible and teachers do not feel obligated to adhere to arbitrary time limits. Some of the teachers encourage the children to choose from among as many as three subject areas during a three-hour morning session. During this three-hour period some pupils work on language activities; others concentrate on mathematics. Still others complete reading assignments. The teacher is more a facilitator than an expository lecturer. He meets with groups of pupils for specific purposes. Often help is given on a one-to-one basis. Teachers sometimes contract with pupils. The pupil agrees to accomplish a designated amount of work in a given amount of time. Pupils frequently pursue cooperative tasks during which leadership evolves on the basis of which pupil is most knowledgeable or skillful in a given subject. Leadership in each classroom is shared among students from the various racial and ethnic groups represented there.

Several State College students have volunteered one or two hours a week to tutor pupils in the basic skills areas of reading, mathematics and language. Included in the tutorial program are some parents who have had experience in some phase of teaching. Teachers feel that the tutorial program is an integral part of our total school program and efforts are being made to expand this program.

A parent advisory committee has been in operation at Fremont School for the past three years. The purposes of the committee are 1) to have a group of people who are better informed of school programs and activities than the average parent and who can act as liaison between school personnel and parents; 2) to provide the school faculty with feedback information from parents relative to the successes and failures of school programs and activities; 3) to provide advice and suggestions to school personnel relative to school policies, and 4) to facilitate cooperation and understanding among parents with differing racial and ethnic backgrounds.

The parent advisory committee meets two or three times a year. It is composed of approximately thirteen parents appointed by the principal, based upon the recommendations of teachers. All teachers attend the meetings. The meetings are conducted in an informal way with open give-and-take discussion being the single most important method of interchange of ideas and information. Classroom visitation is periodically provided for the members of the committee for the purpose of allowing the members to obtain first-hand information about the instructional program.

Each year, prior to the opening of school, an orientation meeting has been prepared and carried out by the faculty for the purpose of informing parents of new pupils about our program. Various members of the faculty prepare ten minute presentations relating to the several areas of the curriculum. Materials are displayed and ample time provided for questions and answers. A tour of the classrooms, library, and learning center is provided followed by a social time over coffee and refreshments. We feel that many problems and misconceptions are averted by this kind of open communication between parents and teachers.

Over the past three-year period the Board of Education has provided approximately $100,000 over and above the normal school budget for the implementation of the model school program. These funds are used to employ paraprofessional aides, provide in-service education, purchase instructional materials and equipment, and finance field trips and other enrichment activities. In addition, approximately $36,000 has been budgeted for transportation.

Program Evaluation

Evaluation of the Fremont program has been the responsibility of the district's testing services department. Control schools were designated in the geographic areas from which some of the children are bused as well as schools in contiguous areas. Both academic learnings and attitudinal learnings have been assessed.

Findings indicate that the pupils taking part in the Fremont program did as well academically as children in the control schools. Fremont students felt better about school and indications are that their own self-images and aspiration levels have improved, particularly among disadvantaged students whose aspirations may be either depressed or unrealistically distorted in segregated environments. Positive interracial relationships generally have been developed by facilitating social interaction and cooperation within an instructional setting that provides for effectively individualized instruction.

XI

Project *Wingspread*: The Chicago Area City-Suburban Exchange Program

Lloyd J. Mendelson and John Bristol

Project Wingspread is a cooperative program through which the Chicago Public Schools and suburban school districts in the Chicago Metropolitan Area expand students' cross-cultural contacts and horizons. Funded under an E.S.E.A. Title III grant, Wingspread makes it possible for city and suburban students, teachers, administrators, and parents to combine their resources and talents in an exploration of metropolitan living. Designed to promote mutual understandings among students of different socio-economic and racial backgrounds, it helps students develop new perspectives about the total metropolitan community.

Students participating in Wingspread attend classes for sustained periods of time ranging from several weeks at the elemenary level to a full semester at the high school level. Using the metropolitan community as the academic setting for realizing the project's goals, students meet with individuals and organizations working toward the alleviation of important urban and metropolitan problems.

Growth of Project Wingspread, 1968-1970

Entrance into the project has been voluntary on the part of participating districts, schools, and students. From its inception during summer 1968 with five central city schools and five suburban districts located in the "North Shore" area, the "wings" have "spread" westward and southward to include thirty-one city and suburban schools during the 1970-1971 school year. Intra-city exchanges involving Chicago public schools of varied ethnic and socioeconomic backgrounds also have been inaugurated. Through June 1971, more than 4,500 students and teachers representing forty-six Chicago and suburban schools have taken part in Wingspread programs.

Programs

Three basic models have been created to implement Wingspread Projects and maximize attainment of its objectives. All three have a shared teaching component with classes composed of both city and suburban students taught by a city and a suburban teacher at a student/teacher ratio of 15 to 1.

Direct School Exchange Pairings

Students and teachers exchange schools for periods ranging from several weeks (elementary) to a full semester (high school). This is accomplished in either a half-day exchange which brings together students and teachers from urban and suburban schools to engage in metropolitan studies units; or, full-day exchange in which visiting students attend the host school in regular classes for one-half of the day, and participate in the metropolitan studies unit the other half of the day.

The direct school exchange is the most dynamic of the models. It affords the greatest impact on the exchange schools and has provided the greatest test of the Wingspread objectives by bringing students and teachers together for extended periods in the participating schools.

The Magnet or Central Site

Pupils and teachers are brought to a central site from three or four schools to provide a varied cultural mix. Either a school magnet site or a community center becomes the base of operations. The central site reduces travel time. The curriculum is similar to the other models. This arrangement has been used only at the elementary levels. It has the advantage of easier organization, but it has the disadvantage of reducing the impact on the total student body of the participating schools.

Once-a-Week Interest Groups

High School Workshops in Theatre Arts have been held on Saturdays and Social Science Seminars have been held during school time for students from paired schools, and have proved successful. The advantages of this model are that it involves more students and more schools at greatly reduced costs, and it has produced the optimum degree of immediate interaction among the groups and sustained the highest level of interest. The disadvantages are that there is relatively little extended interaction, and there is no absorption of participating students into the regular school program.

Staffing and Implementation

The administrative staff of the project consists of a director and four coordinators. The primary role of the staff is to select participating schools and to work with them in developing the concepts of the program. After selection of schools, the Wingspread staff, school administrators, teachers, students and community representatives work cooperatively in developing units of study. Combined efforts in curriculum development result in individualized units for each grouping. Throughout the pre-exchange planning, the staff is responsible for conducting in-service training for participating teachers, assisting in materials selection, arranging field classes, working with school administrators to insure a smooth transfer of students, and informing communities about the project. The administrative staff is supported by a secretarial staff of two full-time workers and one part-time worker.

The Wingspread Advisory Board, composed of representatives from participating school districts, agencies, and organizations throughout the metropolitan area, meets regularly to review the programs of the project and offer suggestions for its improvement.

There is no typical Wingspread program. It is possible, though, to generalize about what happens during the beginning, operation, and culmination of an exchange. Interest in a school's participation in an exchange may originate with students, parents, teachers, administrators or community groups who have heard about the program. Often the original idea for an exchange is offered by the Wingspread staff. Upon the display of concern from a school, the Wingspread staff and other interested persons work to cultivate that interest by attending staff and community meetings in order to explain the program. If enthusiasm for an exchange grows at a suburban school, then the school obtains its Board of Education's consent. Sometimes a suburban Board of Education initiates the contact with Wingspread, then selects the school to participate. Chicago schools already have approval to participate since the program is under its jurisdiction. While all Chicago schools are eligible to participate, a school's involvement is determined by the community, administration, parents, and students of individual schools. As the idea of an exchange grows within a school, either city or suburban, the Wingspread staff seeks a school to pair in the exchange. Factors considered in the pairing include the cultural and ethnic characteristics of the schools and distance between them.

As soon as the schools are paired, the administration and the director of Wingspread determine the grade level and the number of teachers and students. Teachers are then selected for the program and in-service training is conducted for the teachers by the Wingspread staff. Students enter the program on a voluntary basis. Students, parents, teachers, administrators, and Wingspread staff develop the curriculum, gather the materials, and select the field classes. The Wingspread staff works out transportation and other logistical problems.

A unit of study such as "Law in an Urban Society" involves classroom study of related printed and visual material by city and suburban students with field classes in courts, jails, courthouses, judges' chambers, police stations, and the like. The field class and classroom work combine to provide a living-learning experience. As students study together, they get to know one another and not only discuss the topic of study, but discover many things about one another as people. During the exchange, parents of students get together to discuss the program and see what the students are doing. Near the end of the program, an evaluation instrument is devised and given. After the program ends, Wingspread supports follow-up activities such as periodic visits with each school serving as host, with indoor and outdoor activities.

Curriculum and Instruction

The curriculum in Project Wingspread focuses on a study of the various ethnic groups in the metropolitan community. Particular attention in a program is given to those ethnic groups present in the cooperating schools. Emphasis is placed on groups possessing strong ethnic attitudes and the historical and sociological reasons for such developments. Every phase of the curriculum stresses the importance of cross-cultural contributions to the urban community. Data from evaluation instruments indicate that both elementary and high school students have been identifying with the problems of persons who differed from themselves while becoming more aware of their own group's cultural and ethnic contributions.

Wingspread units concentrate on a variety of social, political, economic and cultural resources as the primary tools for learning. Students gain first-hand acquaintance with the institutions and people of the community. The project has developed and is refining curriculum material designed to offer greater student exposure to and information about life in the urban community. Elementary and high school units focus on such topics as:

People of the Metropolitan Community: A study of the cultural traditions, social patterns, contributions, and current problems of ethnic groups in the Metropolitan community.

Problems of Law and Justice in the Metropolitan Community: An examination of the politics of laws and law enforcement.

Public Services in the Metropolitan Community: An investigation of the relationships and interdependence of urban services and urban people.

Dynamics of Urban Change: A look at the economic, social, and political forces causing significant change.

Other units explore ecology, the performing arts, and the industrial element of the metropolis.

City and suburban students, teachers, administrators, and parents have cooperatively developed educational experiences ranging from seminars with college presidents and corporation chairmen to a week of studying plants and animals at conservatories and zoos.

More than 260 agencies and industries in the city and suburban areas have cooperated with Project Wingspread in hosting over 4,000 field classes. Students and teachers have obtained first-hand information concerning the roles and functions of the agencies and industries of the metropolitan community. The flavor and excitement of the learning experiences have been captured very well in the following description written by a former teacher who visited Wingspread classes:

Especially at the high school level, the curriculum units are interesting enough in content, rich enough in unusual field experiences, and challenging enough in questions of concern for our times to make the adult reader envious of the young people who have the good fortune to live them. "Living them" is an appropriate term, for these units are not cut and dried material out of textbooks; they are the stuff of which contemporary urban life is made.

In the unit, "Social Problems in Law and Justice," for example, students read and discuss such basic documents as the Constitution and Bill of Rights, Supreme Court decisions, and legal case studies. But they don't stop there. They also watch our system of justice in operation, in Boys' Court, Narcotics Court, and the criminal courts. They visit suburban and city legislative bodies for a firsthand look at the ways in which laws are created; they tour penal institutions to observe how society punishes its offenders. They discuss rehabilitation with the staff of St. Leonard's House, an Episcopalian halfway house for released prisoners. And they discuss ways of safeguarding our freedoms with staff members of the Chicago office of the American Civil Liberties Union.

Chicago, as the home of many groups of people of differing backgrounds, is the concern of the unit on "Social Anatomy of the Metropolis." In field classes the students come face-to-face with spokesmen of various ethnic, religious, and racial groups. As they visit such places as the DuSable Museum of African-American History, the Ling Long Museum, the American Indian Center, and the Japanese-American Service Center, they see the preservation of differences that contribute to the many-faceted ways of American life. They learn that there is still a need for services for those who are new to the city, and they see these services in operation at the Chicago Southern Center, the Puerto Rican Commonwealth Office, and the Spanish outpost of Hull House, Una Puerta Abierta.(1)

Wingspread:
A Suburban View

Problems and urban living are nearly synonymous. Residents of our cities no longer can live as if they didn't exist. Pollution, drugs, and racial unrest are inescapable. They are so great, in fact, that they can no longer be viewed as only city problems.

The need to introduce suburban students realistically to the problems of urban living is a major educational concern. How can teachers who work in predominantly suburban situations talk about this problem? How can textbooks be selected to deal with the nature of such living? How can students become involved in a meaningful way with the problems, challenges, and resources of urban living?

Project Wingspread offers an answer by making the city and suburbs the classroom, and using business and industry, the courts, and the entire metropolitan area itself as textbook and resource material.

Suburban students are given an opportunity not only to learn about and use metropolitan resources with their peers from the city, but also cooperatively to analyze problems and seek solutions. Corporation executives are confronted by the students with questions on such topics as pollution, social justice, and fair hiring practices. Through these kinds of experiences, students gain a better perspective of the interrelationship of living conditions, job opportunities, police protection, and other aspects of the metropolis. With a broader frame of reference, students become acquainted with a diversity of problems some did not even realize existed.

Many advantages accrue to the suburban school through such a program. How well can we relate to and meet the academic and social needs of a city high school student? How should we react to the concerns of the parents of city students attending our schools?

Students participating in Wingspread are most enthusiastic regarding its importance to their educational experience. Contacts with city youth are maintained after the program is completed, as are interests in the resolution of problems examined through the program. Parents of participants show equal enthusiasm based on the experiences of their children.

An extremely important experience for suburban students is the opportunity to spend a semester in a city high school. The students in fact become members of the city school, attending classes as participants, not as visitors. Unlike most school experiences, this one is real, not simulated. Suburban students who participate in Wingspread find it hard to take a simplistic view about the complex problems of urban education and urban development.

Problems

In its growth and development Wingspread has encountered troublesome areas. The three most persistent sets of problems and some of the actions taken to solve them have been as follows:

Apprehensive City
and Suburban Parents

Parental apprehension usually arises from lack of information about the program. Wingspread attempts to resolve this problem by establishing communications with parents through:
1) pre-organizational explanation sessions
2) parent involvement in pre-planning exchange visits by parents
3) parent involvement in on-going program activities
4) parents assuming leadership in planning parent-exchange meetings during the course of the program

Parents who participate in planning, as observers in the on-going program, as participants, or in parent get-togethers are less prone to be apprehensive about safety, loss of identity, and the academic value of the program. Communication is the key to dispelling fear.

Tensions and Hostilities
Resulting from Racial
Isolation and Stereotypes

Bringing groups of students together from different backgrounds can create points of tension. Potential tension points are anticipated by the staff. These points are worked on before and during the program by:

1) encouraging community identification with the program by involvement in its creation
2) disseminating the program's intent and nature to the students and staff of each cooperating school
3) working toward insertion of the Wingspread program into the regular school schedule
4) encouraging contact between Wingspread and non-Wingspread students and sponsoring supportive activities on the part of non-Wingspread students and teachers

Input from non-Wingspread students and teachers and their communities reduces points of tension and aids in breaking down stereotypes.

Differences in Teaching
Approaches and Attitudes
Toward Learning
Among Teamed Teachers

Administrator and teacher selection and commitment is the key to a successful program. In those programs where the teachers were committed, interested in the students, and capable of teaming with peers, the programs were highly successful. Wingspread works toward the attainment of successful teams through 1) careful teacher selection; 2) a series of in-service training periods; 3) teacher exchange visits prior to the program, and 4) on-going teacher-coordinator-director conferences.

Evaluation

The services of evaluation consultants from the University of Illinois Circle Campus and other institutions have been utilized to develop an evaluation design and direct its implementation. The evaluators have employed a variety of techniques and instruments, including standardized forms, pre- and post-testing, taping of interviews and encounter sessions, and the development of a special instrument titled the Metropolitan Community Attitude Inventory (MCAI). Experimental and control groups were utilized as needed to assess the effects of the Wingspread experience.

Evaluation data collected during the first two years indicated that Wingspread succeeded at several levels.

For 1970-71, evaluation data were collected from four general sources: 1) an examination of previously prepared reports and evaluative data; 2) a questionnaire sent to a representative sample of professionals who had been involved in the project; 3) personal interviews with persons either directly or indirectly associated with the project, and 4) on-site visitations and observations where the project was or had been in operation. Only the questionnaire results are summarized here.(2)

Most frequently reported positive influences on students were in the areas of human relations, attitude formation and respect for individual and cultural differences. Percentages were slightly higher for suburban students.

Regarding positive Wingspread influences on programs, no single influence stood out for suburban schools, while "innovation" predominated for Chicago schools. A larger percentage of blacks reported the project to have a positive influence on student academic achievement than did whites. Suburban respondents reported the project had an influence on attitude formation more frequently than did Chicago respondents. Chicago respondents cited positive influences on teachers, programs, administrators, and parents consistently more frequently than did suburban respondents.

An overwhelming majority (90.7 percent) of the respondents favored the continued operation of the project, with 65.8 percent favoring continuation "as it is now," or "on an expanded basis." Many more favored continued operation as a part of the "regular school day program" (43.6 percent) with "both inter (city-suburb) and intra (within Chicago) exchange programs" (59 percent), than with just "Saturdays and summer programs" (16.2 percent).

In response to an open-ended item which asked the respondent to state some of the negative effects of Project Wingspread, a vast majority among both suburban and Chicago professionals either did not respond or indicated no negative outcomes. Both groups thought there was a need to expand (i.e., involve a greater number of students and schools) and lengthen the duration of project programs.

Problems most often cited by suburban respondents involved

the lack of an understanding of the dynamics of urban students by both suburban professionals and students. Some instances of suburban student boredom were mentioned.

Urban administrators indicated concern for well-trained teacher substitutes as replacements for those teachers away from their regular duties while involved in Wingspread activities. There was also some concern expressed regarding the stereotyping of urban students by their suburban counterparts.

In spring 1970 a follow-up study also was conducted at the high school and upper grade levels to determine the impact of the program on former participants. The following quote represents the evaluator's summary of the follow-up:

On the whole, as contrasted with the initial evaluation, the children a year later talked much less of specific field experiences and much more of the understandings and awareness that were the after effects of these experiences. The majority of children see themselves as more socially aware and attuned to the world around them. They found their social growth, such as making friends, broadening their perceptions of other people, reviewing and modifying their stereotypes, and showing more awareness of themselves and their ability directly related to their participation in the Wingspread program.(3)

Additional
Impact
and Implications

Wingspread's impact has not been limited to temporary effects associated with the various programs it has initiated and implemented. The long-range effects of the project include:

1) Friendships have been established and maintained for more than two years.
2) Follow-up activities and inter-visitations have been initiated by Wingspread students and parents.
3) Wingspread clubs have been formed in participating high schools.
4) Principals report that participating elementary students have shown greater enthusiasm toward schools the following term and in many instances have performed better than anticipated on achievement tests.
5) Teachers report that high school students who have had the semester experience in Wingspread perform well in social science classes the following year, and tend to become more active in student affairs.

Effects extending beyond the project's fundamental programs include the following:
1) Metropolitan Community Studies units are now being used by other programs under the auspices of the Chicago Board of Education.
2) Chicago schools not presently included in the program have requested consideration for involvement.
3) Suburban school districts have initiated credit courses in urban studies based on the Wingspread curriculum.

In this era of racial polarization, Project Wingspread has demonstrated an effective means of establishing communications between people. This has been accomplished without abridging the individual's identity, but rather by utilizing the resources of the metropolitan area as a vehicle to demonstrate that all members of our society have aided its growth and development. Models and mechanisms have been developed for programs which can be effectively applied in metropolitan area schools. Black students, white students, Spanish-speaking students, Oriental students, students from every ethnic group in the urban area have participated in the exchanges and have gained a better understanding of what it means to live in a modern urban society.

Notes

(1) Maryell Cleary, "Wingspread: Where People Are People," *American Education,* April 1971.
(2) Although the distribution of the questionnaire was not wholly random, every effort was made to obtain a stratified sampling according to location (city and suburb), grade level (elementary and high school) and Wingspread model (paired exchange, magnet site). To facilitate collection of information, project coordinators collected the completed questionnaires in sealed envelopes from the participating schools. Thus 155 out of 166 or 93% were returned.
(3) Harriet Talmage, "Summary of Follow-up to 1969 Upper Grade Junior High Exchange," Board of Education (Chicago: 1970), pp. 8-9 (mimeographed).

XII

From Model
to Practice:
Guidelines for
the Effective
Implementation
of Interracial Programs

Daniel U. Levine

To provide a constructive interracial experience requires much more than simply choosing or devising a suitable model and obtaining the needed funds. Issues involving implementation have been discussed as appropriate in several of the preceding chapters. Most of the points discussed may seem self-evident to teachers and administrators who have experienced or thought deeply about such problems. Basic principles of program implementation, nevertheless, seem to be ignored at least as often as they are honored in practice, as can be amply demonstrated by visiting schools and talking to teachers in desegregated schools in almost any city. In this chapter a set of guidelines is proposed for use in implementing the kinds of programs described in the preceding chapters.

1. Programs designed to provide positive interracial experience should be based on social-psychological principles known to play a part in determining whether interracial contact will have a positive impact on intergroup understanding and relationships.

Interracial contact does not automatically result in better intergroup relationships. In many cases interracial contact not only fails to have any positive effect on attitudes and behavior but actually serves to heighten intergroup hostility and conflict. A desegregated high school which is constantly in turmoil, for example, may compound rather than reduce tendencies to engage in interracial stereotyping and scape-goating. Positive interracial experience, in other words, does not just happen whenever people of differing races are brought together in the same building with little or no attention to the nature and quality of their interactions.

An excellent brief statement summarizing the state of current knowledge concerning intergroup contact has been provided by Israeli psychologist Yehuda Amir in a paper reviewing the results of many research projects. Several of Amir's conclusions could well serve as a statement of planning goals for the wide variety of interracial programs described in this book:

There is increasing evidence in the literature to support the view that contact between members of ethnic groups tends to produce changes in attitudes between these groups.

The direction of the change depends largely on the conditions under which contact has taken place; "favorable" conditions tend to reduce prejudice, "unfavorable" ones may increase prejudice and intergroup tension.

Some of the favorable conditions which tend to reduce prejudice are a) when there is equal status contact between the members of the various ethnic groups, b) when the contact is between members of a majority group and *higher* status members of a minority group, c) when an "authority" and/or the social climate are in favor of and promote the intergroup contact, d) when the contact is of an intimate rather than a casual nature, e) when the ethnic intergroup contact is pleasant or rewarding, f) when the members of *both* groups in the particular contact situation interact in functionally important activities or develop common goals or superordinate goals that are higher ranking in importance than the individual goals of *each* of the groups.(1)

2. Interracial learning experiences and environments should be carefully planned in advance.

Regardless of whether interracial contact occurs in the corridors or on the playground, in clubs, athletics, or other activities that are part of the co-curriculum, or in academic settings as part of the formal curriculum, one fundamental principle applies in each situation: students do not automatically develop intergroup understanding merely by being left "free" to interact with one another. The goals of intergroup learning are achieved consistently only when appropriate learning experiences are provided as part of a process that includes careful specification of goals and step-by-step evaluation of results. Terry Borton has given many examples of this generalization based on years of classroom experience building an affective curriculum that might help students better understand themselves, their relations with others, and the world in which they live:

> . . . I was stuck between the alternatives of a jazzed-up English curriculum which turned students on but gave them nowhere to go, and simply giving them the freedom to express themselves. I had stretched the English curriculum about as far as it could conceivably go and still retain the title; the notion of simply providing more freedom did not seem to meet the needs of the kids either. . . . A few students seemed to need that kind of room, but most needed more than being tossed out on their own. They needed help; they were asking their teachers to teach.(2)

3.   Interracial education programs cannot be successful without substantial in-service staff development efforts.

A few simple guidelines are suggested here to govern staff development efforts in preparation for programs of interracial education.

   a.   All members of a faculty, including paraprofessionals, secretarial staff, and particularly administrators, must be involved in the training program.

   b.   Top-level administrators not only must participate fully in the training program but must totally accept and support its objectives.

   c.   Except for occasional departures such as a weekend retreat, training sessions must be part of the regular working week and must be scheduled for blocks of time long enough (e.g., three hours; half-days) to achieve important purposes.

   d.   Training sessions must be held regularly over an extended period of time. Certain points in a training program, for example, may require a half-day every week or a full week once every other month for an academic year.

   e.   Attention must be given to helping participants acquire *both* the attitudes and the classroom teaching techniques necessary to implement a given instructional program successfully.(3)

   f.   A substantial portion of time must be set aside for developing problem-solving skills and for enabling the entire faculty to function as a group in solving the problems that impede the implementation of a given instructional program.

   g.   Resources needed to achieve the goals of a particular instructional program must be made available and capability in utilizing them properly must be developed as part of the training.

    h. Training must include adequate provision for continuous
follow-up assistance offered at least partly in actual
classroom settings.

4. Effective implementation of an interracial education program
requires fundamental changes in the organization of the school and
the scheduling of the school day.

A faculty that expects to achieve the goals of an intercultural or
interracial education program merely by squeezing a few parts of it
into a traditionally-organized school might as well forget about the
whole idea. A productive discussion on race relations, for example,
cannot often be carried on within the confines of a forty-or fifty-
minute hour, to be abruptly and artificially ended when a bell
rings. A faculty, similarly, cannot fruitfully work together to solve
problems or plan an effective instructional program if its members
are allowed to work together for only an hour or two once or twice
a week. A group of students cannot derive much benefit from a
field trip which is promptly forgotten in the regular round of
classes or from working on a common project which brings them
together in very large groups for only a few minutes a day. Unless
the goals to be achieved govern the schedule to be followed, interracial relationships and contacts will be superficial. Little will be
accomplished to overcome the defensiveness, naivete, and hostility
produced among both blacks and whites by 300 years of slavery
and segregation. Integrated school programs which go this route,
not surprisingly, tend to generate racial bitterness and upheaval
rather than improved interracial understanding and cooperation.

5. Successful interracial education requires outstanding administrative leadership.

There is no question but that interracial education programs
frequently will flounder and perhaps even blow sky high without
outstanding administrative leadership. When Murphy formulated
his well-known "law" predicting that "Anything that can go wrong,
will," he very well may have been thinking particularly about integrated schools in the big cities. Unless the building administrator
and his staff exercise unusual initiative and good judgment,
problems in interracial education programs easily can accumulate
to a critical level and then mushroom completely out of control.

To prevent this, and to achieve the goals of interracial education, administrators must set up workable problem-solving and
feedback mechanisms throughout the school. In addition to monitoring progress and problems in all aspects of the program and ensuring that every student and teacher has representation in
decision-making, administrators often will have to make important
decisions without waiting for direction from the central office.

Problems which arise may run the gamut from working with teachers who behave or are perceived as behaving too leniently (or too harshly) toward either white or black students, to dealing with unauthorized visitors who are creating real or imagined disruption within the school. In some cases teachers may have to be transferred from one position to another with little advance warning; in other cases, groups of parents, students, or teachers may need to be reminded in no uncertain terms about the rights of other parties in a dispute. In no case should one rely on an average administrator to muddle through, if only because there is so much less room to cover up for an ineffective program than there is in the typical homogeneous school.

6.   Interracial education programs must be solidly based on a sophisticated philosophy of choice within pluralism.

A philosophy of "choice within pluralism" is one which aims to help each person acquire the skills, knowledge, and attitudes to interact comfortably with other people of different racial or cultural background. Some individuals will tend to move primarily within a racial or ethnic ingroup, some will participate primarily in heterogeneous groups of varied racial and ethnic composition, and some— probably the majority—will participate at times in each type of group. The ultimate goal must be to make sure that choice is not limited because individuals lack the experience or resources to work with others who differ in racial and cultural background. This goal cannot be accomplished unless participants in interracial education programs directly and honestly confront issues involving race, social class, and cultural pluralism, without retreating into canned formulas that conveniently substitute slogans for choice. What made the experience of one integrated summer school uniquely valuable, as Terry Borton has described it in *Reach, Touch and Teach*, was that the students enrolled were explicitly told:

'Here it is, it's all yours. What are you going to do about it? You've got to make your lives together work in this situation. You're protected from the outside and you've got to work it out.' When they tried to run away, we told them they were running away. And when they became militantly integrationist, we told them they were running away. We were saying, 'How are you going to make it work, so that people are just people or so that people are just people with particular kinds of backgrounds and assumptions and feelings?'(4)

7.   Attention and resources must be devoted to helping students who have special learning problems and/or accumulated deficits in academic skills.

Because desegregated student populations frequently show an

unusually wide range of variation with respect to content, quality, and adequacy of previous academic preparation, many will need special help in acquiring basic academic skills needed to function successfully at a given grade level. Low-income black students who have attended segregated inner city schools typically are retarded one or two grade levels in academic performance by the time they reach the fifth or sixth grade. Attendance at a school serving students most of whom live outside the inner city can help low-achieving inner city youngsters make up a substantial proportion of this gap. Although some may improve in academic performance merely by attending a non-inner-city school, progress will be most marked and widespread when special assistance is provided to overcome individual learning problems.

To the greatest extent possible, such assistance should not be given in a context that singles out a group of students for special treatment but should be an integral part of a school-wide program to provide individual help in learning for every pupil.

No set of guidelines for implementing an educational program is worth very much unless some individual or group insists that the guidelines are followed in practice. Without outside help in monitoring and identifying problems, resources tend to be spread thin and vital prerequisites for successful implementation tend to be skipped over or ignored. Formal evaluation emphasizing continuous collection of data and reporting of results is obviously a necessity if pitfalls are to be identified while they are small enough to be circumvented or eliminated. It is desirable also to involve parents and other citizens in every stage of a program from planning through evaluation and to provide them with enough access to information so they can help identify failures in implementation as early as possible.

Many of the programs described in this book have devoted substantial resources to evaluation and/or have organized governing boards which play a major role in setting policy and in advising program administrators. Good intentions generally are evident in proposals for providing young people with interracial educational experiences, but the history of schools is replete with the wreckage of educational programs that made no special provisions to ensure effective implementation. Wherever the road paved only with good intentions may be thought to lead, it is not usually to the destination its sponsors had in mind when they labored long and hard to get it built.

Notes

(1) Yehuda Amir, "Contact Hypothesis in Ethnic Relations," *Psychological Bulletin*, Volume 71, Number 5 (May, 1969): 338. Quoted by permission. One valuable resource for teachers who wish to utilize the principles of social psychology in providing positive interracial experience in integrated groups or classrooms is the recent paperback book on *Group Processes in the Classroom* by Richard A. Schmuck and Patricia A. Schmuck (Dubuque, Iowa: Wm. C. Brown, 1971).

(2) Terry Borton, *Reach, Touch and Teach. Student Concerns and Process Education.* (New York: McGraw-Hill, 1970), p. 61. Quoted by permission. This book, with its many examples of classroom activities designed specifically for improving intergroup and interracial understandings, is a basic source for anyone planning to implement an interracial education program.

(3) An excellent set of guidelines for conducting in-service training to bring about attitude change is provided in James A. Trimble, "Sensitivity: A Superintendent's View," *Educational Leadership,* Volume 28, Number 3 (December, 1970): 268-269.

(4) Borton, *op. cit.*, p. 51.

Related Professional Books from

Charles A. Jones Publishing

Curriculum Improvement for Better Schools, Jack R. Frymier, Ohio State University, and Horace C. Hawn, University of Georgia, 1970.

Behind the Classroom Door, John I. Goodlad, University of California, Los Angeles, M. Frances Klein, Institute for Development of Educational Activities, Inc., and Associates, 1970.

Toward Improved Urban Education, Frank W. Lutz, editor, Pennsylvania State University, 1970.

The Impact of Negotiations in Public Education: The Evidence from the Schools, Charles R. Perry, University of Pennsylvania, and Wesley A. Wildman, University of Chicago, 1970.

Humanistic Foundations of Education, John Martin Rich, University of Texas, 1971.

Guiding Human Development: The Counselor and the Teacher in the Elementary School, June Grant Shane, Harold G. Shane, Robert L. Gibson, and Paul F. Munger, Indiana University, 1971.

Innovations in Education:Their Pros and Cons, Herbert I. Von Haden, Miami University, and Jean Marie King, Alachua County, Florida, Schools, 1971.

Early Childhood Education: Perspectives on Change, Evelyn Weber, Wheelock College, 1971.

Charles A. Jones Publishing Company
Village Green   698 High Street
Worthington, Ohio 43085